the POWER
of BLESSING

Terry and Melissa Bone

To Dave,

Go into all the
world Dave!
See you in
Afghanistan!

Terry & Melissa
Bone &?

Table of Contents

Foreword

M y wife Ann and I both felt the same way after attending an inspiring teaching series led by Terry and Melissa Bone for our staff at Crossroads/100 Huntley Street. We concluded that this special couple must come back and bring to our TV viewers the same insightful, life-transforming message of *The Power of Blessing*. During the teaching sessions, Ann and I frantically scratched out as many notes as we could (hers were legible) while wishing we could have simply picked up the book...but it didn't exist yet! We later encouraged Terry and Melissa to share their God-given wisdom in book form, in addition to their continued on-the-road seminar ministry, thus enabling a much broader and more lasting impact. And I'm so glad they did!

You are holding a resource that I know God will use to open your eyes to the truth of how specific blessings at pivotal points in life have a profound bearing upon the discovery of your personal identity and destiny. I had never before understood how clearly these principles are revealed in the Bible, especially as experienced by Jesus during His life on earth. Since gaining these new insights, Ann and I are now seeking ways to practice *The Power of Blessing* in our family. I encourage you to read these pages prayerfully, and then ask the Holy Spirit for wisdom in the application of these powerful principles for you and your loved ones. Get ready for miracles!

Ron Mainse
President,
Crossroads Christian Communications Inc.

Acknowledgements

We would like to thank publicly certain people who helped us discover, and share with others, the life-giving truths contained in this book. We are deeply grateful to:

Craig Hill
(Family Foundations International) For pioneering the concepts of seven crucial stages of blessing;

Alf Davis
For friendship and wise counsel when we needed it most;

Rolf Garborg
For believing in us when he hardly knew us;

The Lakemount Worship Centre
And its leadership team for allowing us to practise on them for many years;

The Crossroads Centre Team
Especially Gary Gerard, Ron Mainse and Norm MacLaren for coaxing us to record this message in book form and for making it available to the nation;

Daina Doucet
Whose skill in editing is surpassed only by her patience with novice writers.

Introduction

Blessed be the God and Father of our Lord Jesus Christ who has blessed us with every spiritual blessing in the heavenly places in Christ.

Ephesians 1:3

I n more than 20 years of serving in various forms of church leadership, we were constantly challenged by the reality that many people cannot seem to receive or retain the truth of God's personal love for them. While most of us can appreciate the concept with our intellect, too few of us seem able to apprehend the reality in our heart.

We were also challenged by the reality that we were not much better off than the people we served. And so we embarked on a personal journey to discover the keys to wholeness based upon God's revealed Word.

Somewhere along this journey toward emotional and spiritual health, we stumbled across the understanding of the power of blessing. We found that blessing worked restoration much more quickly and effectively than anything we had ever before experienced. Understanding and applying blessing as taught and modeled in Scripture radically and permanently altered the way we counselled, ministered and related to others.

The Bible speaks of many kinds of blessings, both material and spiritual. They range from blessings people bestow upon God, to God blessing our implements of work and worship. This book focuses on what we call The Family Blessings – those that convey the personal impartation of identity and destiny.

After having learned the seven stages of blessing, we studied Scripture and discovered these stages in the life of Jesus as recorded in the Gospels. Suddenly, as if we had put on a new pair of glasses, new insights concerning the role and power of blessing leaped off the pages. We discovered that from His conception until His baptism Jesus was the recipient of needed blessings that the heavenly Father brought into His life through others. It soon became apparent that if Jesus needed these blessings in order to fulfill His destiny on earth, then we would too!

The Family Blessings refer to the words, deeds and ceremonies that confer heaven's favour upon our identity and destiny. They are our birthright as children of God. With them we prosper despite our weaknesses. Without them we struggle even though we may be gifted. As Ephesians 1:3 clearly states, they are stored up for us in heaven, purchased by Jesus, and ready to be distributed to us at key moments throughout our entire lives.

When you arrived on earth two special people were assigned by God to give you those blessings at each stage of your development. The technical term for these people is "parents." Most of them did the best they could, but very few understood the role and power of blessing during their children's formative years.

The resulting bad news is that all of us have missed some of God's intended blessings during our life's journey.

The good news is that it's never too late to recover missed blessings, or to pass them along to the next generation.

This book will help you to understand the blessings every person needs, how to get the ones you have missed, and how to give blessing to the ones you love. The best news is that it may be a lot easier than you think!

May Ephesians 1:3 be yours!

Terry and Melissa Bone
I.D. Ministries

We Bless You

We bless your ears, that you may hear the message in this book because it is written for you.

We bless your mind, that you may understand the truth about your unique Identity and Destiny.

We bless your spiritual life, that you may feel the presence of God as you discover the depth and breadth of God's personal love for you revealed in these pages.

CHAPTER ONE

What Is
This Power?

*Words of blessing spoken in the name of God are
somehow able to transmit the power and favour of God.*
Rolf Garborg[1]

*I pray that out of His glorious riches He may strengthen
you with power through His Spirit in your inner being.*
Ephesians 3:16

We left the church astonished at what had transpired.
We had witnessed a demonstration of life-changing
spiritual power that evening, and here's how it happened.

We had decided to attend a mid-week service at a local
Anglican church where we knew the minister well and
appreciated his sincere faith. At the end of the service he
invited everyone forward for prayer. Terry responded and
knelt at the far end of the row of people lining the altar.
After serving communion and anointing each person with
oil, the minister turned to Terry and asked, "Now would
you anoint me and bless me?"

Seeing the sincerity in his eyes, Terry leaned over as they
knelt, laid a hand gently on the younger man's head, and
spoke forth good things that we knew about him and his
ministry. Immediately an overwhelming sense of God's pres-

ence surrounded them. Through tears Terry affirmed the calling and the sense of destiny that we could both see in this man from having watched him grow in his role for several years. As Terry spoke the Holy Spirit gave him words about the special future God intended for this man's ministry.

But there was one thing Terry didn't realize. The entire congregation had shared in this personal moment of blessing. Their intimate exchange had been transmitted via the minister's lapel microphone to everyone. As Terry returned to his seat, he could see how deeply others had been moved by the words. In addition, we later learned that the young minister had been fasting and praying for understanding on certain issues. Apparently the words of blessing were an answer to his prayer.

How could something as simple as a blessing yield such powerful results? We had only said a few words affirming the man's character, expressing his value, and picturing a special future for him. Yet as we spoke, many felt a visitation of God in the room. We continued to feel the impact of God's presence as we walked the few blocks home.

The power of blessing

What is blessing? In it's simplest terms, blessing can be understood as God's favour being poured into a person's life. Words of blessing impart life and hope, and change the way we think about ourselves.

Blessing conveys heaven's perspective on who we are and where we are meant to go in life. It invites the Spirit of God to download heaven's spiritual resources into our hearts.

Blessing is already yours

It may surprise you that God has already provided you with all your blessings. Ephesians 1:3 says God "has blessed us with every spiritual blessing in the heavenly places in Christ." It's as if innumerable "packages" of blessings are stored up for us in heaven's warehouse. All of them have been paid for through the sacrifice of Jesus, and contain vital provisions for successful living. Each one has been personally prepared and individually labelled. And many of these packages have your name on them. However, there is one small technicality. The blessings are in heaven and we live here on earth. The important question is, how do they get transported from heaven to earth?

"Blessing conveys heaven's perspective on who we are and where we are meant to go in life"

Through words! Words we speak are vehicles that transport spiritual blessings from heaven to earth. They transform the promises of God from potential in heaven into power on earth.

Many Christians have discovered the power of words by claiming God's promises from His Word through what is known as a "prayer of faith." Often prayers of faith are directed toward receiving things we need – like health, a home and finances. For example, a person may affirm through declaration that God will meet all their needs according to His riches in Christ Jesus (see Philippians 4:19).

It's exciting to see prayers of faith use the power of words to get things from the God who loves us. But it's even more exciting to watch how blessing harnesses the power of words to give things to the ones we love. Also, Scripture emphasizes that we *give* blessings, rather than *claim* them. Many times throughout His Word, God commands us to bless others. If we eagerly obey these commands, then we also receive the blessings God has intended for us.

Since the time we began to understand and teach this revelation, we are constantly encouraged, and frequently amazed, at the positive changes we see in people's lives. Here is a short sampling of typical results.

Blessing affects whole families

A friend of ours who runs a ministry to the homeless was surprised by the power of blessing. Ron[2] had never met his birth father. Then Ron's ministry was featured on television. His birth father watched the program, and for the first time realized who his son was, and what he was doing with his life. This man immediately called Ron and blessed him telling him how proud he was of what Ron was doing. Not only did those words fill a life-long vacancy in Ron's life, but from the time Ron shared the story with his son, their relationship experienced sudden improvement. Ron now eagerly passes on blessing to his son as well.

Blessing is key to family reconciliation

In our walk with Christ we are taught that we must forgive people who hurt us. Obediently we choose to forgive, only to discover that our emotions still reflect the pain resulting from the hurt. It becomes a struggle, at times, to bring our emotions in line with our will. We have found that the emotional side of forgiveness is much easier to attain when we are blessed.

While we were teaching a seminar on blessing at a mission school we discovered that one student was at a point of hating her life. Her mother had died in a car accident, and her father had moved to another country while she was in her teen years.

During the seminar she learned that parental blessing is important for a successful journey through life, and that if one hasn't experienced that blessing, one can feel cheated and angry. She connected her own anger with the fact that she had missed blessings from both parents. During times of personal ministry we helped her recover them. Two months later we received a letter from her saying she was going to visit her father. The letter was signed, "Living for God and loving it!"

In another instance, a middle-aged couple who heard the teaching on blessing realized they had never been blessed by their parents. After our ministry team helped them recover the missed blessings, they undertook blessing the husband's parents. The impact was profound. The father opened his heart and enabled a family reconciliation just before his death.

Blessing is a door to locked hearts

In one city, after we taught the stages of blessing and ministered to those present, a woman who had attended wrote to say that for the first time in 30 years as a Christian she had felt God's love. Until then, she had simply believed by faith that God loved her. Rather than seeing herself as "just a forgiven sinner," she now saw herself as uniquely cherished by a God who lovingly formed her from her mother's womb.

Blessing conquers self-doubt

One individual constantly felt unsure of himself although he had a very successful ministry. After identifying and receiving the blessings he had missed, he testified to a "new, conquering self-confidence." He now mentors young adults.

Another young man to whom we ministered didn't think he would be a good father. Over the course of a few years he discovered, and recovered, blessings he had missed. He now has three children whom he and his wife bless every night. You can feel the joy when you enter their home.

Blessing brings a sense of belonging

A youth pastor confessed that even though he was in full time Christian ministry he had never felt that he belonged with other leaders. When he heard us teach about the stages of blessing, he realized that at a particular stage of life he had failed to receive the needed blessings. After receiving personal ministry, he enthusiastically announced that for the first time in his memory, he felt as if he belonged.

Another young adult who was adopted shortly after birth told us, "When you blessed me with the father's blessing, I felt free from the blockages in my life. I never had another man step into the void from my birth father and bless me like you did. I can truly say there was breakthrough...I now feel complete."

These are a few of the testimonies that we receive regularly about the life-changing power that touches people through blessing.

Blessing fixes what life has broken

There is a way of helping people enter into wholeness without them having to spend years in counselling. While Bible-based, Spirit-filled counselling is a gift from God for every pastor and his congregation, we have agonized over the snail's pace at which many of our folks progressed through traditional forms of counselling. Eventually we discovered that the slow process of getting better is rapidly increased when people learn to understand and receive missed blessings.

Blessing is a main theme in the Bible

Yes! Blessing is totally biblical! Blessing is mentioned more than 300 times in the Bible, and more than 60 times in Genesis alone – the book of "beginnings." In the first chapter of the Bible, Genesis 1:28, God blesses humankind. In the last chapter of the Bible, Revelation 22:3, God again blesses the human race, this time with complete restoration and removal of all curses. In between God weaves the story of how He promised and delivered blessing across four generations to Abraham's family and purposed to return blessing to all the families of the earth.

The Bible is all about blessing. And today God is restor-

ing the understanding of how to give and receive the blessing He has already purchased and stored up for anyone
who believes in Christ.

Endnotes

[1] Garborg, Rolf. *The Family Blessing,* p.32. Word Publishing. 1990.
[2] Names are changed, unless otherwise indicated, to protect the privacy of
parties involved.

CHAPTER TWO

Blessing is the Answer - What is the Question?

So God created people in His own image; God patterned them after Himself; male and female He created them. God blessed them and told them...fill the earth and subdue it.
Genesis 1:27-28a NLT

Thus conscious that I do exist, In time's eternal plan; O grant that I may know at least, Why I was made a man.
Thornton Hayward[1]

We live in the beautiful Niagara Peninsula, about 30 minutes drive from one of the main border crossings between the U.S.A. and Canada. Like four million other Canadians in the area, we often find ourselves traveling between the two friendly nations for a variety of reasons. Whenever we approach the uniformed officials in a booth at the border, we know we will have to answer several questions. The journey is delayed until we provide believable answers. The first two questions always have to do with our identity: What is your citizenship? And, Where do you live? For some reason, when we tell them the answer they never take our word for it. They want proof. It sure helps to have a passport!

But that's not all. Two questions sure to follow are more difficult to prove: Where are you going? and, What is your

9

purpose for going there? Until we convince the stern-faced official that we really are going where we say we are going, we won't get across the border.

The same is true in life. There are key transition points in everyone's life journey at which we must stop and address the questions: *Who am I?* and *Where am I going?* Our life's journey is delayed until we provide satisfactory answers.

Discovering your true identity

Who am I? This question has to do with identity – the sum total of who you are. Your identity is what makes you unique in this world. Before we come into relationship with God, our identities are largely a product of our family experience, our personality and choices we make. But as we come to know God and submit to His transforming work, our identities are reshaped. Boy, have you changed! a friend may say to a new believer. Which one, then, is the real you?

> *"God designed you to be blessed. At each stage of life, you deserved to receive a full measure of blessing."*

Your true identity is the one that God has purposed for you – the one tailor-made just for you.

Did you ever hear about the man who purchased an off-the-rack suit on sale even though it was five sizes too big? When asked how it fit, he replied, "The jacket is fine, but the pants feel a little loose around the armpits."

Trying to be someone God has not purposed for you to be is like wearing a suit that's not made for you. It may look great on the rack, but when you put it on it feels awkward or looks silly.

Terry has a tailored suit purchased at great cost by a generous friend who sent him to a well-known tailor. All Terry had to do was choose the fabric and allow the tailor to measure him meticulously. Weeks later when Terry returned, the tailor, who remembered him by name, disappeared into the back room and reappeared holding a three-piece suit that fit only one person in the world. That suit was not only made from the finest fabrics, but every detail of Terry's frame had been taken into consideration. It felt right and fit comfortably because it was expertly made just for him. It also looked so much better than something off the rack.

Understanding who you are in God is like putting on a designer outfit made just for you by an expert. You feel good about yourself just the way you are. You know you are important and valued.

Discovering your divine destiny

The next set of questions you must answer at key transition points in life are: *Where are you going?* and, *What is your purpose for going there?* After all, your destination defines the purpose of your journey.

The word "destination" comes from the same root word as "destiny." It is defined as a predetermined course of events to which a person is assigned by fate. While that is true for one who does not know God, your destiny in God is far more secure. It isn't like a suit off the rack assigned by an impersonal power called "fate." Yours is the "designer" version. God has pictured a special future for you and pre-planned exactly what He intends for you to accomplish in life. He also wants to reward you for fulfilling your destiny once your life is done. Not a bad deal at all!

If we are secure in our identity, but unsure of our destiny, then we will be delayed, or even denied permission to move on at the "border crossings" in life. So, what are those border crossings, and how do we discover our true identity and destiny so that we may find safe passage?

Seven border crossings in life

Author and pastor Craig Hill describes seven crucial times when blessing is required to impart a sense of identity and destiny[2]. In our ministry we have found that these "crucial times" are truly the border crossings of our life's journey where we must address important questions in order to cross successfully into the next phase. We have also found that these questions are not answered until we receive specific blessings pertaining to each stage.

The only two people on earth who didn't need blessing to move from one phase of life to another were Adam and Eve. They were uniquely different from the rest of us. They were, in fact, the only two people without belly-buttons! In other words, because they were not born, they were not subject to the stages of life. God imparted the full measure of blessing to them in their full-grown state.

Everyone since Adam and Eve, including Jesus, was born into the world through a woman's womb. A full understanding of identity or destiny isn't imparted to us in a moment's time as it was for Adam and Eve. We acquire knowledge of our destiny more gradually as we progress through the major stages of development, from conception, pregnancy and birth, through early childhood and teen years, and on to adulthood and senior years.

At each stage God has assigned certain persons, especially parents, to bless us through words, deeds and ceremonies. These blessings become divine deposits in our hearts, and represent essential affirmation about who we are and where we are going. When we possess them in abundance we prosper in life without striving. When they are absent, we struggle in life in spite of our valiant efforts.

Blessings at the border crossings

How do we know if we have been sufficiently blessed? We have developed a series of life-questions that correspond to each stage. These questions will help you determine the divine deposit of blessing you need in your soul and spirit at each developmental stage so that you can mature into your rightful identity and destiny.

Stage of life	Major life-questions
1. **Conception**	Am I welcome in this world?
2. **Pregnancy**	Is there a safe place for me in the world?
3. **Birth**	Will my needs be met in this world?
4. **Early Childhood**	Who can I trust in this world?
5. **Teen Years**	Do I have what it takes to make it in this world?
6. **Adulthood**	What am I called to do in this world and who will share my journey?
7. **Senior Years**	Am I still needed in this world?

Conception: *Am I welcome in this world?* We like to say that your life begins on your "earth" day (day of conception when your spirit arrives on earth – see Chapter 8), rather than on your birthday. Therefore the first time you need a blessing is the moment the announcement comes that your mother is "expecting."

Seeds of rejection are sown at conception. How you were conceived and how your parents received the news of your conception are powerful factors in shaping your sense of identity.

Think of your first day at a new school or church. You immediately need to be recognized and welcomed. Feeling unwelcome affects your entire experience afterward. In the same way, your little being needed a warm welcome into this world when you arrived here for the first time.

Pregnancy: The second time we need a blessing is during our months as a pre-born child. *Is there a safe place for me in this world?* we ask.

The fear factor in life taunts us even before our birthday. Recent studies provide evidence of a fact most mothers perceive intuitively – that pre-born children are affected by their mother's emotions, whether good or bad. The home environment and the mental, physical and emotional states of a mother serve to answer this life-question for the baby she has not yet met.

Birth: *Will my needs be met in this world?* demands a newborn. Before you understood your parents' language, you learned from experience. How you were held, touched, fed; the words you heard, and the manner in which they were spoken, taught you whether or not your needs would be met in life.

Early childhood: A child reaching out to others asks, *Who can I trust in this world?* From a toddler, through to a preteen, you learn which relationships are safe and which are not. A foundation of basic trust needs to be poured into your personality during those years for you to grow in relationships later in life.

Teen years: Puberty brings the biggest transition from conception. At the beginning of your teen years you need to know, *Do I have what it takes to make it in this world?* This question is a powerful driving force that must be answered so that you can develop the kind of emotional maturity and confidence that will make it possible for you to accomplish your calling in life.

Adulthood: For the past few years we have ministered to many young adults in various countries. The question we are asked most often is, *What am I called to do in life?* A companion question arises: *Who will share my journey?*

Many people are married to someone who does not share their spiritual journey. Creating and maintaining shared dreams and hopes for the future can be an elusive goal. For those who are single by choice or circumstance, God intends to provide good friends who understand them and share the dream of who they are to become.

Senior years: Everyone who has reached their senior years needs to know that they are still needed. Thus the question, *Am I still needed in this world?* In biblical times elderly people stopped working in the fields and took up positions of honour in the city gates. This was a place of authority. Once they reached this stage in life, they were valued not for what they did, but for who they were, and for their wisdom. Our seniors today also ought to be valued for what they know and who they are, and not just for what they do for others.

As we encounter each of these major life-questions, they continue with us for life. If a question remains unanswered, we are drained of emotional energy and sapped of spiritual strength. We feel like a leaky bucket that requires constant refilling to maintain the water level. If a question was answered negatively, we build protective walls within our heart. Unfortunately, walls designed to shut out pain also keep out love.

As a result, questions not answered adequately become emotional baggage we drag along throughout our journey.

For instance, a person may suffer from a sense of not belonging. They might also tend to respond with fear and have a hard time trusting people. In their innermost being this person may not be sure they "have what it takes" to succeed in their highest dreams. To top it off, they might have married someone who doesn't express much interest in their journey. What an enormous amount of baggage to carry while trying to determine and fulfill a destiny!

Perhaps you don't find it hard to imagine this scenario. Maybe you even identify with some of these feelings. There is hope! But it is important to realize that major life-questions aren't answered in one day or through a single event. Answers are assimilated at each stage and are reinforced throughout life.

What is the ideal answer to each question? A blessing! God designed you to be blessed. At each stage of life, you deserved to receive a full measure of blessing. Yet the people God assigned to ensure you receive all He has intended for you may have let you down. That's inevitable. Everyone misses some blessings. The good news is that it doesn't matter why or how you missed them. It's never too late to recover them. Let's find out how.

Endnotes

[1] Hayward, Thornton. *My Plea.* An unpublished poem from the Bone family archives.

[2] Hill, Craig, *The Ancient Paths,* p.69. Family Foundations Publishing, 1992.

CHAPTER THREE

Living Without the Blessing

When Esau heard his father's words , he burst out with a loud and bitter cry and said to his father, Bless me – me too, my father!

Genesis 27:34

Few people see themselves as struggling with missing out on their family's blessing, but people around them see it.

Gary Smalley & John Trent[1]

E sau was more than 40 years old. He was a married man with children of his own, yet he wept like a little child because his father would not lay his hands on his head and bless him.

Esau knew the stories of God's promise to Abraham his grandfather. He was aware of how God had appeared to his grandfather and to his father, and he longed for the day that the blessing God imparted to them could be passed on to him. Esau was grief stricken at the thought of trying to live the rest of his adult life without it.

Why was blessing so important to Esau? What did he know about blessing that most of us don't?

He knew that without the blessing he would have no access to the rich storehouse of promises made to his grandfather Abraham.

He knew that without the blessing he would not prosper in spite of his talents.

He also knew that *with* the blessing his brother Jacob would prosper in spite of his faults.

And so he wept. He wept for what could have been but now was beyond reach.

Through Jacob, Abraham's family blessing continued to be passed on through generations and centuries. Under Moses' leadership, God mandated many practices and procedures for the children of Israel that included various kinds of blessings for families at all stages of life. Those blessings not only secured their identities within them, they also raised protective walls around them keeping them safe from the enemy's schemes and curses. Even Balaam, who was hired to curse Israel, found himself unable to do so. Every time he opened his mouth he heard himself blessing Moses and the people of God (see Numbers 22, 23). The walls of a generational blessing surrounded and protected them from any attempt to curse what God had blessed.

Each one of us needs these walls around us. Proverbs uses the metaphor of a walled city to describe a person's emotional life: "Whoever has no rule over his own spirit is like a city broken down, without walls" *(Proverbs 25:28 NKJV)* (see also Psalm 80:12).

In biblical times, whenever there was a break in the wall of a city, all productivity came to a halt. Every worker in the city became a warrior. Each one laid down implements of industry and picked up implements of war. Instead of *thriving,* all energy was consumed in *surviving* (see Nehemiah 4).

How many people do you know who spend most of their energy struggling with problem after problem – paying insurmountable bills, dealing with broken relationships, handling rebellious children, and perhaps struggling with physical sickness? No time and energy is left in their lives for serving God. Why are they struggling with continual affliction and suffering more than they deserve? Because their protective walls of blessing are broken down. They may never have been built in the first place. They may be paying the price for generations of neglect.

But when blessing is properly passed on and built into a person's life, it forms walls of protection so that "soul" energy can be used for productive living rather than protective behaviour. *You cannot "rule" in life until you are blessed* (see Genesis 1:28).

Few of us today value our parents' blessing the way Esau did, however when we do not have their blessing and approval, we are subject to a longing that cannot be fulfilled any other way.

A poignant illustration came in a letter from Laura who told us she had waited all her life for a blessing from her father. From her earliest years she had tried to please him to no avail. Carrying his tools to the construction site at the tender age of eight, she didn't win his approval. Nothing she did worked. Each time she failed to measure up to his expectations, he responded with verbal abuse.

As Laura grew through her teen years she tried even harder. Having scored 97 percent on a high school exam, she proudly presented her paper to her father. "Where are the other three marks?" he demanded. From that moment, everything changed.

Totally defeated, she gave up. Something within her died. Until age 25, Laura was caught in a downward spiral of alcohol and broken relationships. When she became a Christian, her behaviour changed, but she confessed that 25 years later she still had a longing deep inside to hear the words "well done" from her father.

Laura experienced more personal pain when her husband died suddenly. For the next year she managed to keep her household running as a single mom. Although her 82-year-old father had not provided any support for her during her personal loss, 12 months later he surprised her with a phone call to tell her that he was proud of how she had taken care of everything in the past year.

Rather than being resentful, Laura was thankful. She had finally received a small taste of what she had longed for all her life. She told us that the phone call from dad "was like a cool breeze on a hot summer day, or a sip of water when I'm parched. I waited so long to hear those words, and I am so thankful they were spoken before he died."

Making up for loss

Whether we realize it or not, we tend to adopt certain relationship patterns in an attempt to compensate for missed blessings. The way we relate to others has a discernable "bent" in one of three ways. This is best illustrated by the experience of a woman we encountered at a retreat. She told us that the teaching helped her understand why she and her two sisters were so different from each other even though they had experienced the same family misfortune. In her own words:

> Our father was very conniving. Always wanting a boy, he undermined us as growing women. I got angry. My tendency now is violent anger toward any hurt or injustice. The second child is so in agreement with the identity put on her, that to this day she has bouts of depression requiring her to take a few days off at a time just for restoration. The youngest went a different direction. She has read all the books on self-improvement and has determined to be the nicest person out there.

Her story illustrates the three basic personality patterns that people unwittingly adopt in an attempt to compensate for the lack of parental blessing: aggression, agreement, or compensation.

Aggression: People become aggressive when they are attempting to reject the rejection they have experienced. They may become defiant, stubborn, cynical, and critical of others, and may reject authority, or refuse comfort. In essence, they are trying to "fight fire with fire." The unfortunate result is usually a bigger fire. The fact is you can't solve criticism with a critical attitude. You can't cure the pain of cursing by cursing others.

> *"Without blessing, we are the walking wounded, carrying within us pain from the past while we try to get on with our lives"*

Agreement: People who come into agreement with the lack of blessing will think thoughts of inferiority and failure. They might also suffer from anxiety and low self esteem. You can recognize this kind of person by the way they constantly put themselves down with their own words. For people who live in such a state, the devil doesn't even need to exist – they are doing his job for him!

Compensation: Those who compensate for the lack of blessing can become performance oriented, constantly striving, compulsive, self-centered and self-absorbed. In spite of great achievements they often remain emotionally immature.

Many people from religious homes compensate for missed blessings by doing good works because people affirm them in their good works. The doers of good works believe that their drivenness is pleasing to God. Such is not the case. The Bible makes it clear that we do not earn God's favour through our efforts.

Others compensate by making light of their situation, like a young married woman who came to us for counselling. With a forced laugh she said, "My family puts the 'fun' in dysfunctional." This woman was always laughing, but we could tell by her story that her life had actually been no laughing matter.

We applauded her efforts to overcome the obvious hurt, but covering the situation with a humorous attitude (or any other attitude) couldn't bring healing and wholeness to her life.

Detoured destiny

When people are missing the blessing upon their identity, they will be delayed or detoured in their search to discover and live out their destiny. They will spend their days constantly striving to attain self-inspired goals. They may achieve great accomplishments, but will not fulfill the unique purpose designed for them by God. If they don't slow down and realize what's missing in their life, they may never be able to experience the joy of "ruling" in the area of life that God has reserved just for them.

While obviously dysfunctional homes have problems that can block the blessing from reaching family members, other types of home environments can also be detrimental. A person doesn't necessarily receive a full measure of blessing just because they grow up in what seems like a "good" home.

Children with a strong religious upbringing may remain fiercely loyal to parents who strive on the surface with "applaudable addictions" – excellent behaviour, good works, and tireless effort for a noteworthy cause. Yet underneath the parents are driven by an unseen need for love and approval because they have never been properly blessed. As a result, the blessing is blocked from reaching the children.

After a workshop, a pastor wrote:

You described people who felt they had missed out on their father's blessing. My dad was a great pastor...he loved the ministry, and gave everything to the church. However, he never took any time off for his family.... I eventually forced him to take a day off work.... On that day he still got dressed in a suit and tie, went to his office, read books about pastoring, and slept with his feet on his desk.

The pastor recalled that, although his mom had done her best to compensate for his father's absence, years later when he was driving his father to a nursing home, the pain he felt at losing all hope for a meaningful relationship with his dad was "indescribable." His mother's efforts couldn't make up for the lack of his father's blessing. Tragically, his father passed along the deficit from his own life. As a result, for most of his life this man functioned under the inherited burden to please people, until God healed that part of his character.

Without blessing we are the walking wounded, carrying with us pain from the past while we try to get on with our lives. But unlike Esau, you do not have to spend the rest of your life in remorse over what could have been – not when you discover how blessing works.

Endnotes

[1] Smalley, Gary & Trent, John. *The Blessing*, p.125. Pocket Books, New York N.Y. 1990.

CHAPTER FOUR

How Blessing Works

Say this to Aaron and his sons. This is the way you shall bless the children of Israel. Say to them, The Lord bless you and keep you; The Lord make His face to shine upon you and be gracious to you; The Lord lift up His countenance upon you and give you peace. So shall they put my name on the children of Israel and I will bless them.

Numbers 6:23-27 NKJV

The Ancient Hebrews recognized that words of blessing spoken in the name of God are somehow able to transmit the power and favour of God.

Rolf Garborg[1]

In 1953, three technicians at the San Diego Rocket Chemical Company were assigned to develop a water displacement compound that would prevent rust and degrease missile parts in order to prolong their life and function. It took them 40 tries to invent the formula, so they named the new product "WD-40®." The formula has remained a carefully guarded secret known only to a select few.

When the company learned that employees were sneaking the product out of their facilities to use at home, they decided to package it in aerosol cans and sell it to retailers. Now millions are benefiting from this invention.

WD-40®'s amazing diversity and practicality are demonstrated by this excerpt from a list of favourite uses compiled on the 50th anniversary of its invention:

- Cleaning hands
- Keeping rust from forming on tools and saw blades
- Protecting silver from tarnishing
- Removing the squeakiness in door hinges
- Removing oil spots off concrete driveways
- Removing grease and grime from a stove or grill
- Restoring and cleaning chalkboards
- Removing tomato stains on fabric
- Lubricating bicycle wheel sprockets
- Removing lipstick stains
- Keeping bathroom mirrors from fogging
- Protecting the Statue of Liberty from the elements

And, most unusual, someone discovered that it keeps flies off cows.

WD-40® has also been designated as the "official multi-purpose problem-solver of NASCAR" (an auto racing association).

Approximately 2.5 million gallons of the stuff are produced and sold each year because it works, and because it is simple to use. You don't have to be a rocket scientist to point the can at the problem and spray. For a vast array of applications, it has the remarkable ability to displace gunk and restore the item to its proper use.

Better than rocket science

We like to say that blessing is WD-40® for the soul. It has amazing diversity and practicality. You can apply it to a variety of problems in life because it has the remarkable ability to remove unwanted "gunk." When blessing is applied to an area of need, we almost immediately find ourselves functioning more like God intended. It is supernaturally effective, and it doesn't take rocket science to know how to use it because we don't need to be trained counsellors to bless people. In our opinion it ought to be designated as the "official multi-purpose problem solver of the kingdom of God."

For some, like Kim, blessing puts fun back into life.

Kim had lost her sense of enjoyment in the regular routine of married life. Afraid to fail, she had been taking herself and her life too seriously. As a result, she had developed a lack of interest in cooking. After she had received blessing, she experienced a discernible change in her attitude. Her excitement for cooking returned. She and her husband had pure fun experimenting, and she was able to laugh at her failures. In her own words:

> *Your blessing teaching is definitely working for me. I feel very enthusiastic. After 23 years of marriage I really feel like cooking. I collected recipes off the Internet, and started to experiment. After my first try, the smoke alarm sounded. I asked my husband to take it to the back room. Since then I've learned so much!*

Fascinated with the effect blessing had had on her own life, she continued:

> *One of the girls at church told me that after the Blessings Workshop, her husband has changed. He has become closer to their daughter...a definite and obvious difference....*

And then Kim asked a very important question:

> *I wonder, what makes it work?*

The power of words

How does blessing work? Unlike the three scientists who developed WD-40®, The Father, Son and Holy Spirit have not kept their formula for blessing a secret. On the contrary, the principles of how blessing works are revealed and modeled in Scripture.

Blessing instills honour and value through words, deeds, and ceremonies.

Words say it;

Deeds show it;

Ceremonies seal it.

We like to describe it this way:

Blessing is the divine delivery vehicle that delivers the goods from heaven's storehouse into your life. Honour and value (personal worth) are the goods it delivers, and words, deeds and ceremonies are the roads upon which it travels.

Words carry spiritual authority: Every visible thing originated from that which is invisible; everything we see and touch came from something that we cannot see or touch. And it all came into existence in response to words. God's words created the world that affects us every day in every way.

Words also gave order to the created world. When God first spoke the world into existence it was "without form and void" *(Genesis 1:2).* The wording in the original Hebrew indicates that before creation everything was formless, confused, empty, and a chaotic mess – a bit like our lives feel sometimes. With words God created order out of this chaos. Blessing gives us the ability to do the same with the chaos in our lives.

A characteristic that distinguishes us as humans from every other created being is our unique ability to convey our thoughts, feelings and ideas through the spoken word – language. God imparted this power to humankind. God told Adam to name all the animals. Why? Did He run out of ideas for names? No! God wanted to share His authority through the spoken word with humans. While God's words created every creature, Adam's words gave each one an identity.

Words have the power of impartation: Words can cheer us up or wear us down. Words can change the way we think and the way we look at ourselves. "The tongue has the power of life and death..." *(Proverbs 18:21).*

All words are powerful, but the most powerful words of all are those that convey blessings. Whenever you permit someone with relational influence in your life to speak words of blessing to you, God works in agreement with those words and makes a spiritual deposit into your soul.

More than thirty years ago, Terry was a young teenager and a brand new Christian. One evening after a youth meeting, the man assigned to drive the kids home reached over as Terry got out of the car, placed a hand on his shoulder, looked him in the eye and spoke four words from his heart: "Bless you, my child." The sincerity was obvious and his actions validated his words. However, there was something even more to them than just a heartfelt wish – there was spiritual impartation. Those words touched a deep need within Terry's heart for love and affirmation. Terry still remembers how valued and important he felt at that moment.

Words of blessing can alter the world around us. The words used for blessing in the Bible illustrate this point.

In Old Testament Hebrew the word *berakah* means the transmittal of God's favour.

In New Testament Greek the word *eulogeo* means to commend with excellence of language. *Eulogeo* is also the root of the word "eulogy" which refers to the verbal tribute we bestow on someone after they die. Unfortunately, at a person's funeral it's too late to give them a blessing.

God gave Aaron the high-priestly instructions for blessing the people of Israel (see Numbers 6:23-27). We call this the Aaronic blessing. It has been used in many Christian churches for centuries.

The Aaronic blessing was a corporate blessing to be given to the entire nation on a regular basis – perhaps even daily. Thus each time Aaron repeated these words, he stood in front of the tabernacle and faced thousands of tents. He knew that if he spoke the words of this blessing, God would invest it with the power of His Spirit and agree to favour the nation by protecting them from their enemies and providing for their needs.

> *"Blessing is the divine delivery vehicle that delivers the goods from heaven's storehouse into your life"*

In the process, the very character of Jehovah was stamped upon the people of Israel (see Numbers 6:27).

Aaron was appointed to facilitate the blessing upon an entire nation with his words. But what if the person whom God has appointed to stamp His character upon you failed to do so for some reason?

Undelivered blessings

The good news is that God can, and will use anyone He chooses to deliver a blessing to us. Even if they don't know us well, God can give them the understanding to speak the appropriate words of blessing.

A powerful example is found in the life of Abraham. God promises to bless Abraham, to make his descendants a great nation, and to give him a land forever (see Genesis 12:1-3). Abraham believed, but he hadn't yet received. Though full of faith, he was still an old man walking through a land he didn't own, without the children God had promised him.

But along came a man named Melchizedek (see Genesis 14). This man didn't just pray for Abraham to be blessed; he blessed him with the words that God gave him. Abraham already possessed the promise, but not until God sent the right man did he receive the blessing that activated the promise (see Hebrews 7:6).

It appears that Terah, Abraham's father, had also been destined for the promised land of Canaan (see Genesis 11:31), but died *en route*. It could be that when Melchizedek affirmed Abraham's destiny, he was standing in the place of Abraham's departed father.

Many of us have believed God's promises for our lives without receiving them. Since it is true in Abraham's life that the covenant promises began to unfold only after he received Melchizedek's blessing, it can be true for us as well. Blessing is the key to receiving them.

Some people try to claim their blessings by an act of faith. After discovering the biblical power of blessing, one man told us that he flew to his home country and read the Aaronic blessing to his 90-year-old father saying, "I know you don't believe in the Bible, but lay your hands on my head and say these words so my life will be complete." Unfortunately, that man will find that demanding a blessing from someone who should have given it, doesn't always work. For a blessing to have full spiritual impact, the person giving the blessing must be willing to do so, and must understand the words that need to be spoken in relation to the identity and destiny of the person receiving the blessing.

Children in blended families can experience blessing when the parents understand the needs of their children and what to speak into their lives. We received a very touching letter from a mother and step-father who, after attending a Blessings Workshop, decided to bless their "special needs" son – a 21-year-old functioning at a much younger age mentally. The mother wrote:

My husband and I had a very special time with our teenage son.... I was separated from my first husband at about the half way mark in my pregnancy with my son. It was such a difficult time.

My husband and I cried out to God and then we talked to our son. We had tried to explain things to him over the years, but his understanding is not deep.... He knows he was three when we got married, and... that there was another dad, but he also knows that my husband is his dad. We prayed through the stages of development with him and my husband blessed him in those stages.... Our son says that he feels different now, but he doesn't know how or why exactly. Wow! God is good, and the blessing is so powerful.

These wise and loving parents discerned that due to the history of their blended family, their son had not received blessing at every stage of his development. By carefully crafting their words and accompanying them with much prayer, they spoke words of blessing over their son, and the Spirit of God backed their words by downloading something into this young man's spirit even though his mind couldn't quite comprehend what had happened.

The New Testament confirms that someone else can supply blessings you might have missed. Often, during Jesus' earthly life, the people closest to Him were unable to bless Him appropriately. Father God made the provision by bringing others alongside Jesus to speak blessing at crucial moments (more about this in later chapters).

The power of deeds and ceremonies

Deeds and ceremonies validate memorable moments of blessing in our lives with actions that reinforce the sincerity of the words spoken. They impart spiritual power. When planned well by parents and family members who choose to honour our wishes by keeping our best interests in mind, events such as birthdays and weddings offer a wonderful opportunity to back up words with actions. Another interesting ceremony planned by some parents is a "blessing party" that welcomes teenagers into their teen years – a Gentile version of the Jewish *bar mitzvah*.

However, it doesn't always take a major event to validate a blessing. It can be sealed with a brief and informal ceremony as well. Like signing for a package delivered to your home, validating a blessing through ceremony brings closure to the transaction and proof that the goods have been delivered. We will never forget how a simple ceremony altered the course of a young man's life.

At a conference where we had ministered to hundreds of pastors and missionaries, a young man in his twenties approached us. We listened to his story and performed a simple ceremony. We stood in the place of his mother and father, and asked him to place all his insecurities symbolically in a box. Then we asked him to walk toward us. As he came into our arms, we spoke many things to him about his character and calling that were evident to us through personal observation and reports of his excellent reputation. He shares the impact this celebration made:

In my walk with God there seemed to be something that I had not been able to attain. I felt that there was a root of some kind in my life and realized that it had to do with not having my father's blessing. For whatever reason, my father withheld his blessing from me for as long as I can remember. When I shared with my parents that God had called me into ministry, my mother was excited, but my father, because of his past, did not bless me (he had left the ministry).

When you performed the simple ceremony of calling me forth into my adult destiny, I felt...the ground was bro-

33

ken to the 'new pipeline' of blessing.... It was a powerful experience.... I was able to see the moment with Jesus in the room. Jesus was the one giving me His blessing.

In our culture we don't really have an occasion when a father calls his children forth and blesses them, but it is so necessary.... Many things occurred in those moments. I have now begun a journey of discovery. For the first time in my life I am beginning to understand who I am. Since that day I have a new, conquering confidence.

Jesus received His Father's blessing before he launched out in ministry, not after. My life is shifting from attempting to earn a blessing, to being blessed by my true Father.

God just happened to put us in the right place at the right time to speak the right words into this precious person's life. Today this young man has a nation-wide ministry and enjoys mentoring young adults in their search for identity and destiny. That's how blessing works.

Endnotes

[1] Garborg, Rolf. *The Family Blessing*, p.32. Word Publishing. 1990.

CHAPTER FIVE

The Family Blessing of Abraham

I will make you into a great nation and I will bless you; I will make your name great, and you will be a blessing. I will bless those who bless you, and whoever curses you I will curse; and all peoples on earth will be blessed through you.

Genesis 12:3

The blessing of a father builds houses for the sons. The blessing of a mother fills them with good things.

Rabbi Jesus ben Sirach

It was the ultimate power encounter. As the crowd on Mount Carmel watched with anticipation, the 400 prophets of Baal failed miserably trying to get their god to perform a miracle. Elijah, the lone prophet representing Israel, stepped forward for his turn.

How would you address God in a moment like that?

We would likely pray: *Oh God,* who parted the waters of the Red Sea for Moses...; or, *Oh God,* who demolished the walls of Jericho...! We would try to build our faith through recalling the mighty works of God. But Elijah stepped forward and prayed, "O Lord God of Abraham, Isaac and Jacob..." *(1 Kings 18:36).*

Elijah didn't rely on precedent. He relied on covenant – the covenant God made with Abraham. *A covenant of blessing!*

God's promise to bless Abraham and his family, to prosper them throughout the generations, and to curse those who curse them, was a stronger faith builder for Elijah than any single miracle. He knew that the source of his own miracle-working power was derived from the strength of that inter-generational blessing.

Every Hebrew in Bible times knew the story of Abraham's family intimately. They grew up hearing their parents tell stories over and over of how the blessing was passed on from Abraham to his great grandchildren. They, in turn, became the patriarchs of the tribes that gave identity and destiny to every Hebrew child. They believed God guarded and guided their families. The inheritance of blessing gave them security and significance.

Further proof of the importance of Abraham's family blessing is revealed by the "air time" this story gets in the book of Genesis.

The account of the creation of the universe outside of our solar system gets a total of five words – "He made the stars also" *(Genesis 1:16)*. That's all we need to know about it – God made them! Black holes in other galaxies may be interesting to read about but they do not affect our daily lives.

Meanwhile Abraham's family story gets 38 chapters!

After the account of the flood, the Bible focuses exclusively on the details of periodic events in the lives of Abraham's family because they contain crucial information on how to become blessed and how to pass that blessing on to the ones we love. There is much we can learn from them.

God initiates the blessing (see Genesis 12:1-3): God promised to bless Abraham, his family and his descendants. He said He would favour and prosper them and make them into a great nation that would affect world history.

In God's promise to Abraham, the two words "I will" stand out. They are repeated five times. God is the one who initiated the promise to bless Abraham and his family, and when He made a promise, He delivered. Abraham didn't have to earn the blessing, but he did have to believe and obey in order to acti-vate it. Abraham and his descendants also had to be careful to ensure that they passed on the blessing to sub-sequent generations (see Genesis 12:2-3).

> *"Abraham didn't have to earn the blessing, but he did have to believe and obey in order to activate it"*

Melchizedek blesses Abraham (see Genesis 14:19-20b): The identity of the mysterious Melchizedek is a favourite Bible study topic, but Scripture makes it plain that we do not know his personal identity. However, it is also plain that Melchizedek knew Abraham's identity and therefore was able to bless him. Scripture seems to include only a brief summary of what Melchizedek said, but it is clear that Abraham was favoured by God and that his enemies could not prevail against him.

Knowing who Melchizedek was is less important to us than knowing what he did. The lesson here is that God uses people to bless people. Many of the promises of God for our lives would be fulfilled more readily if they were released through a proper blessing by someone who knows our identity and destiny.

Abraham's blessing is confirmed with Isaac (see Genesis 26:2-6): Abraham passed his family blessing on to Isaac with the result that Isaac's major life decisions were guided by God's personal counsel. The power of that blessing, confirmed here personally to him, protected him from major detours in the pursuit of his destiny. Although this blessing was handed to him as a gift from God, Isaac had to choose to walk in its light. Each subsequent generation faced a similar challenge. None could walk in blessing until they willingly participated in the faith of their fathers.

Isaac prospers because of the blessing (see Genesis 26:12): Isaac's diligent work in planting seed in the fields for harvest received a supernatural boost. God blessed him with a hundredfold crop increase in the first year. God will also prosper our work, or business venture, when we walk in the covenant blessings.

Isaac is so blessed that even his enemies bless him (see Genesis 26:28-29): As the saying goes, "If you can't beat them, join them." Isaac's enemies failed in their attempts to frustrate Isaac's success by plugging the water holes essential to sustain his flocks and herds. On more than one occasion he gave them the well and moved to another place where God blessed him with an even greater supply because "the blessing of the Lord brings wealth, and he adds no trouble to it" *(Proverbs 10:22)*. Realizing that they could not hinder Isaac from prospering, they changed their tactics and decided to enter into a peace treaty with him. Isaac did not fight his enemies, yet he overcame them.

When we walk in blessing without resisting those who criticize us, then we can expect God to fight our battles for us.

Jacob "steals" a blessing (see Genesis 27:1-30): Jacob and his twin brother Esau were victims of a struggle between their parents Isaac and Rebekah.

Mom preferred Jacob, while Dad preferred Esau. Isaac was old and almost blind. Rebekah unwisely ignored protocol and dishonoured her husband by urging her son to pretend he was Esau. Her actions revealed her lack of trust in God and caused great trouble for the family.

Jacob deceived Isaac into pronouncing a blessing over him, but Scripture doesn't indicate that he received the full blessing of Abraham. The blessing failed to mention the promised land and the nation of descendants to follow. These words Isaac added later (see Genesis 28:3-4). Thus we can conclude that Isaac had never intended to bless Esau with this aspect of the blessing. The blessing that Jacob stole was one designed specifically for Esau. Jacob had come into possession of a blessing that did not, at that moment in time, reflect his character or the fullness of his calling.

Esau cries out for the missed blessing (see Genesis 27:34-38): Esau was desperate for a blessing, but Isaac believed that once given, a blessing could not be revoked. He gave Esau a secondary blessing that did not adequately reflect the longing of his son's heart. Esau became embittered and full of resentment toward his brother. The result was a tearing apart of family relationships.

Jacob gets Esau's blessing (see Genesis 28:1-15): Interestingly, just before Jacob fled for his life, Isaac added to his blessing. He imparted to Jacob the blessing of his father Abraham – the promise to multiply his descendants into a great nation and to give them the promised land.

Thus a study of the blessings reveals that Isaac had intended to transfer the patriarchal responsibilities and blessings to Jacob even though he favoured Esau. If Rebekah and Jacob had not conspired to steal Esau's blessing, Esau would have been content with the blessing Jacob stole.

Jacob was the chosen candidate for Abraham's family blessing all along. By choosing to manipulate and deceive, Jacob was no more blessed than he would have been had he waited for the blessing that God had intended for him. Instead he added much trouble to his blessing – trouble that plagued him for years. God was willing to confirm His covenant of blessing to Jacob, but nevertheless Jacob had sown deceit, and therefore he reaped deceit from Laban.

Jacob's presence blesses Laban (see Genesis 30:27-30): The fact that tricky old Laban experienced a measure of blessing on his life because of his alliance with Jacob is a powerful truth to watch in action. Laban evidently became convinced of the power of blessing through his association with Jacob and attempted to emulate the blessing with his own children (see Genesis 31:55).

Laban's actions trouble Jacob (see Genesis 29-31): From being tricked into marrying two wives, to being falsely accused of dishonest business practices by Laban's sons, Jacob was repeatedly troubled by Laban's deception. Jacob was now a man caught between an inherited blessing and an earned curse. While God blessed him in his business, the enemy attacked him in his family life with strife. He reaped deception because he had sown it.

Jacob wrestles with the "man" (see Genesis 32): The night of Jacob's struggle was the crucial turning point not only for Jacob, but possibly for all subsequent generations.

Here Jacob had finally escaped Laban's influence. He made peace with Laban, and using a rock as a symbol, they both agreed to keep their households completely separate from each other. Believing his family problems were now resolved, he resumed his journey. But no sooner was he underway when he learned that his estranged brother Esau was coming toward him from the other direction. The last words Esau had spoken to him were, "I want to kill you." It put him in an awkward position.

The unknown "man" – an angel, or perhaps Jesus Himself – and Jacob wrestled through the night. By morning they were discussing blessing. Perhaps Jacob had asked why he had had so much trouble in life even though he was blessed. Perhaps he learned that trouble followed him because he hadn't reconciled family relationships after stealing a blessing that wasn't rightfully his. Whatever direction the conversation took, by early the next morning Jacob's encounter with this heavenly being produced in him a renewed passion for the blessing. He received it immediately. As a result God ended the long-standing family feud and the brothers reconciled.

Jacob's name is changed (see Genesis 35:9-10): God blessed Jacob's identity again when He changed his name from Jacob which means, one who takes the place of another, to "Israel," meaning, one who strives with God and prevails. In doing this, God removed a life-long stigma from him and bestowed great honour on him.

Potiphar is blessed because of Joseph (see Genesis 39:5): The family blessing was now operating in the next generation with a positive effect on Joseph's "master."

Although much trouble awaited Joseph, ultimately, the family blessing, combined with his obedience, preserved Jacob and his sons from starvation. Their survival enabled the blessing to be passed on to the children of Israel.

Jacob blesses his grandsons (see Genesis 48:9-20): In a redemptive act, God allowed Jacob not only to pass the blessing of Abraham on to Joseph, the son who for years he thought was lost, but also to Joseph's sons, Ephraim and Manasseh.

Jacob blesses the patriarchs (see Genesis 49:1-28): This is the grand finale of the book of Genesis. The sons of Jacob became patriarchs of the tribes of Israel. The reunion of Joseph and his brothers was deeply moving. All the incredible events in Joseph's life had prepared him for this one occasion. In fact, the events from Genesis 12 to 48 culminated in this moment.

What enabled these events to take place? The blessing! The *right* person laying his hands on the *right* people saying the *right* words as God directed by His Spirit.

Jacob paid a high price to give the family blessing of Abraham effectively to his sons and two grandsons. The deception in Jacob's life had been forgiven, removed from his character, and forgotten. Relationships among his sons had been restored. Jacob had become Israel, and was now able to discern and declare destiny – an essential ability for passing on a family blessing. In blessing his sons, he shaped a unique blessing for each one and spoke to each, one at a time, about their individual identities and destinies. Yet he did not play favourites.

Although Jacob had much with which to bless Joseph, he reserved the prophetic announcement of the coming Saviour for Judah, not because Judah had earned it, but because God had purposed it to be his destiny. Jacob's God-given task was to call forth their destinies into existence with his words.

The good news is that like Jacob, you too can overcome past failures in order to release a blessing that is so powerful, it will keep on influencing your children and their children long after your work on earth is done.

CHAPTER SIX

Blessing in Your Family

He redeemed us in order that the blessing given to Abraham might come to the Gentiles through Jesus Christ....

Galatians 3:14

To ensure a blessing is fully received, a person needs five positive messages for every one negative message spoken to them.

Alf Davis[1]

Here is some thrilling news – Abraham's family blessing is not limited to those who are his natural descendants (see Galatians 3:14).

Jesus' sacrificial death not only purchased our entrance to heaven, it also gave us access to the same family blessing God promised Abraham. Through that promise you have the right and privilege to receive and give blessings that will change lives today and affect coming generations.

How about your family? We all know the history of the home in which we have been raised. However, not too many of us know much about the generational history of our family. Has blessing been blocked in your life because something happened in your family of origin? Regardless of how far back the blockage began, if you missed out on blessing in your childhood home, then you need to recover that blessing.

Why do I have to look back? Frequently, when we teach about recovering missed blessings, people ask us, "Why do I have to look back over my life?" It's an honest question.

Some say, "Isn't it all under the Blood?" referring to the Blood of Jesus that takes away sin. In the words of Craig Hill, "Sometimes it's just under the cork."[2] In other words, until you pop the cork, the thing that is bothering you will remain bottled up inside, inaccessible to the grace of God.

> *"...if you missed out on blessing in your childhood home, then you need to recover that blessing"*

Others quote Philippians 3:13, "Can't we just forget what lies behind?" It's true that you can forget what lies behind – the event. But you can't ignore what lies beneath – the pain.

It's like hitting a severe pot hole in the road when you're driving. Later you may experience car trouble due to that event. To go back and try to fill the pothole won't help your car. The damage is under the hood.

Likewise, the experience is in the past, but you still carry the damage and suffer from the effects of events long ago that have prevented blessing from flowing in your life.

Steven Covey, in his book, *The 7 Habits of Highly Effective People,* lists self-awareness as the first and most important aspect: "Self-awareness enables us to stand apart and examine even the way we 'see' ourselves."[3]

We need to examine the way we see ourselves. Who wrote the script we follow in life? Why are we following it?

Until we stand apart for a moment and take a look back,

we may never comprehend where and how we can improve our lives.

John, a full time evangelist, attended a conference where we were speaking. After personal ministry he shared his story.

When his mother discovered she was expecting him, his father-to-be wanted her to have an abortion and verbally abused her for allowing herself to become pregnant. From childhood through his young adult years, John frequently experienced failure and rejection. By the time he attended the conference, John had been a Christian for more than 20 years. Although his ministry was very fruitful, none of his own adult children were serving the Lord.

He heard about the stages of blessing, and for the first time he connected his troubled childhood with the failures he had experienced as a father. He realized that he had failed to bless his children due to the missed blessings in his own life. After he repented, John and his wife crafted blessings from Scripture for each of their children and spoke them aloud each day. Even though the children were not present to hear their daily confession, God heard, and He agreed with their words.

A year later, again at one of our conferences, John and his wife couldn't contain their smiles as they announced that there had been significant reconciliation in the family and that all five adult children, plus two spouses, were now serving the Lord!

John discovered that *you can't give what you haven't received*. Looking back, the enemy of his soul had written part of the script for his life. After he allowed God to rewrite that script with blessing, his family life changed.

Words bring honour

Blessing and honour go together. We are told that around the throne in heaven worshippers shout, "Blessing and honour" *(Revelation 5:13)*. Give one, and you receive the other.

In the Bible, the Hebrew word for honour, *kabed,* means, to be made heavy, or to be made glorious, while the Greek word, *timao,* means, to estimate, or fix the value; to prize.

When we honour someone, we place a value on them as a person, and we convey that value through words, deeds and ceremonies. Rolf Garborg, author of *The Family Blessing,* spoke the Aaronic blessing over his children every night before they went to sleep for more than 20 years. The sense of importance, value and worth that was communicated to the children has never left them. Today his children, now grown, continue the practice with their children. The family will likely continue the tradition for many generations to come.

We honour someone when we refuse to judge their feelings, when we listen to their point of view with sincere interest, when we tell them how valuable they are to our lives, when we make birthdays and other important occasions truly special, and when we take time to understand and speak their language of love. This is how it ought to work in families, but often it doesn't.

Words bring dishonour

Many of us have experienced the power of negative words that have dishonoured us. The Bible says that "reckless words pierce like a sword" *(Proverbs 12:18),* and some of us carry those wounds throughout life.

Negative words "curse" a person's identity rather than bless it. We understand a curse to be the opposite of a blessing. A curse therefore brings dishonour, and devalues a person through words that are untrue and unkind.

Any lie that gets past the gateway of our mind and slips into our heart can become embedded in our soul. If we believe that lie, it becomes as powerful as truth would have been in shaping our self worth, causing a detour *en route* to our destiny.

We have observed that without affirmation, correction feels like rejection. Correction given without affirmation will curse a child's identity. Jokes, put downs and sarcastic remarks can intentionally, or unintentionally, cause lasting damage to a person's sense of identity. Often overlooked by parents, constant teasing from siblings can block blessing in children's lives too.

To illustrate correction without affirmation, we like to use the following analogy.

A woman sees a $300 dress in a store window. She goes away hoping that it will be put on sale. Two weeks later she returns, and to her surprise the dress has been marked down every day since she left, and is now $19. But now she is reluctant to purchase the dress for even a fraction of the price she might have paid previously. A doubt has entered her mind: is there something wrong with the dress that she cannot see? Why has it continually been marked down? she asks. What she once considered valuable, is now suspect of being damaged goods.

> *"without affirmation, correction feels like rejection"*

Likewise, some children have grown up in a home where harsh words are common. For example, week after week, and year after year, a young girl hears words of anger, criticism and perhaps even mocking. Every harsh word is like a "mark down" on her self worth. One day she looks in the mirror and says: There must be something wrong with me that I cannot see. I must be damaged goods. The lie has embedded itself into her heart through constant negative reinforcement. She came to believe it to be true, and it effectively cursed her identity.

Our good friend and counsellor Alf Davis, who has a remarkable record in assisting people in recovering missed blessings, believes that most people need five positive messages for every negative message in order to receive a blessing.

Dishonour – a family trait

Satan cannot be everywhere at once. He overcomes this limitation by setting up schemes in human relationships that serve as "traps" to catch and hold us fast in his grip. The bait in these traps is the desire within our nature to return evil for evil.

A person who has been dishonoured will likely return the dishonour or pass it along to someone else. Soon words of criticism and anger are doing their destructive work, and blessing is effectively blocked in that family situation. These patterns are reinforced over time so that in extreme cases, just being in the presence of people with whom we have a long history of dishonour, can bring immense emotional pain to the surface. Sometimes patterns of dishonour are passed on to children by parents, who in turn pass them on to the next generation. The Bible tells us that "sinful" parental patterns can be passed on for three or four generations, until someone rises up and defeats them with the power of blessing.

Dysfunctional families

No one has had a perfect family. Every family suffers from a measure of dysfunction, although some much more than others.

Every family is founded on a system of relationships that is based on a set of rules for acceptable behaviour. These rules are expressed through often-heard sayings such as, "In this home we always…," or, "What will the neighbours think?" These sayings outline the conditions for membership in good standing. They act as a script for the role that each family member is required to play. The classically dysfunctional home is characterized by one or more of the following rules:

"don't think…"	(don't do as I do; do as I say);
"don't feel…"	(there's no reason to cry);
"don't see…"	(daddy isn't an alcoholic, he's just sick today);
"don't talk…"	(children should be seen and not heard).

Each of the rules of a dysfunctional family is a form of dishonour. A close friend, whom we will call Joan, illustrates this point:

I was one of six children; one boy and five girls. I was the third oldest. Most of my life growing up at home seemed to be characterized by silence – there was very little actual cursing, but definitely no blessing.

My parents' view on child rearing was: children are to be seen and not heard. My father ran the home in a very authoritarian manner and we were not allowed to say no, or to express our opinions, or ask questions.

My mother suffered with depression and anger and always sent us outside or down into the basement. She had very little affection for anyone, and never even said, 'I love you,' until I was 30. My parents never talked to me about the facts of life because that subject was taboo.

My father had nicknames for all his children and he continued to use them even when we were adults. I never liked my nickname. It made me feel small and ridiculed. During my teenage years my father would say 'I love you' occasionally, but his actions didn't support his words. We learned that we had to earn everything we received. I had a huge black hole in my life with all kinds of unpaid emotional bills subconsciously waiting for payment. Not even my husband's love could pay them.

Joan's family was classically dysfunctional – the children were denied the affirmation that is essential for a blessed life, and they were dishonoured because they were not allowed to express themselves verbally. Joan was well into her adult life before she believed that her opinion was valuable. Here's the rest of her story:

> *It wasn't until I attended the seminar and the ministry team blessed my whole life, calling me forth as a woman, that I felt whole, loved and of value. I remember my husband saying just a few days later that he had a 'new wife.' I cannot emphasize enough how great an impact the blessing of puberty and celebration of my womanhood has made in my life.*

Improper sexual activity brings dishonour

Respecting each others' bodies is an essential form of honour and is a prerequisite for blessing to flow in families.

In Leviticus there are lists of do's and don'ts for the children of Israel. When it comes to the list of forbidden sexual activity, Scripture indicates it is forbidden because it brings "dishonour."

Any sexual activity outside of wedlock will bring dishonour to either, or both, of the participants. However, any form of sexual abuse, especially committed against a child, will crush their sense of identity. It is a terrible violation of trust. Every victim of childhood sexual abuse of any kind ought to understand that they are not to blame and that they can be fully restored to God's purpose and design for their lives.

Regardless of your family experience, blessing brings change. Many factors determine the speed at which blessing works. Even a lifetime of criticism can wash away, sometimes very quickly, when blessing is given and received. Other times it takes years for the blessing to soak slowly into the depths of a person's understanding. Establishing patterns of honour, and including intentional times of blessing as part of the fabric of family life, will slowly but surely bring health and wholeness to the ones you love.

A word of encouragement to parents

It's never too late to give a blessing to someone you love. It works at any age and stage in life. If you are a parent, you may want to consider where you have neglected to give blessing to your children.

We ministered to a couple who, at 75 years of age, realized that they had not fully blessed their children because they had missed blessings in their own lives. After they received the blessings in a ministry time, they immediately planned a family gathering to speak prepared blessings over each of their adult children.

Another time, a man in his thirties came to one of our workshops because his mother, having attended previously, had called him to bless him over the phone. She had felt compelled to finish the business of blessing her son's adult identity and destiny. The son, a consultant, had been struggling with a lack of clients. Within days

> *"its never too late to give a blessing to someone you love"*

of receiving his mother's blessing, the phone rang steadily. The son attributed this fortune directly to the blessing he had received, and now wanted to learn how he and his wife could pass on blessing to their young children.

When you understand the pattern for blessing at each stage of life, you too will be able to pass it on.

We bless you

We bless your family heritage, that the promises of God for your family line may be revealed and released in your generation.

We bless your family of origin, that your personal experience may be under the influence of God's grace in order to remove every blockage from your intended blessings. May every unfulfilled purpose for your family begin to be fulfilled in your lifetime.

We bless your descendants to come. May the blessings you receive be passed on for many generations.

Endnotes

[1] Alf Davis is a counsellor with Agape Counselling International.

[2] Hill, Craig. *The Ancient Paths,* pp.19-20. Family Foundations Publishing, 1992.

[3] Covey, Steven. *The 7 Habits of Highly Effective People,* pp.66-67. Simon & Schuster New York, New York, 1990.

CHAPTER SEVEN

The Family Blessings of Jesus

Although (Jesus) was a son, He learned obedience...and once made perfect, He became the source of eternal salvation for all who obey Him.

Hebrews 5:8-9

Jesus Christ is the condescension of divinity and the exaltation of humanity.

Phillips Brooks[1]

Jesus' life – a pattern for our blessing
Through the years we had heard various sermons about Jesus' ministry being a pattern for believers in Christ (see John 14:12). These messages focused exclusively on His ministry from the time of His adult baptism.

One day while preparing to teach about blessing, it occurred to us that Jesus' life, before His ministry began, also provides a pattern for us. What had previously seemed like random memories of Jesus' early years, actually match the first six stages of blessing. Found primarily in the first two chapters of Matthew and Luke, these brief vignettes speak about, and model, how blessing is received in those stages of life.

Jesus – the man
The Bible makes it plain that although He was God while

He walked the earth, Jesus was also fully human. He was conceived and entered the world through a woman's womb. He grew up with a mother and step-father. His mother nursed Him, held Him and helped Him take His first steps. He learned how to speak His parents' language, and eventually studied the Jewish customs and the Torah. In His teen years He helped His step-father in the carpentry trade. He ate and slept, laughed and cried, and was tempted in every way that we are – yet with one essential difference; He didn't sin (see Hebrews 4:15).

> *"Jesus absorbed into His very being the curse that was due us... as a result , we have the awesome opportunity to embrace every missed blessing that God intended for us"*

In spite of being the unique "God-man," from the moment of His conception until His ascension and return to heaven, Jesus had to endure the slow process of growing physically and relationally within the family assigned to Him by His heavenly Father. Jesus was allowed no short cuts in His development from infant to adult.

As He passed through each stage of life, He submitted to every aspect of a healthy family life, including the significant times when He received blessing on His identity and destiny from other people.

Jesus – fully blessed as an adult

Jesus never lost sight of His identity or destiny. He maintained perfect poise while continually meeting challenges to His authority. Immediately after His adult baptism, the devil attacked His identity saying, *"If you are the Son of God..."* *(Luke 4:9)*. You can almost hear the mockery in those words.

In effect the devil was saying, Who do think you are? I have more power than you.

But Jesus knew no lack of security or significance. Even when weak from 40 days of fasting, He could not be turned away from pursuing His purpose.

The next challenge He faced came immediately after the 40-day fast when He suffered rejection in His home town (see Luke 4:16-30). Things got ugly that day. The hatred the people of Nazareth demonstrated toward Him became very personal because they had known Him for years. They rejected not only His message, but also Him as a man. They cursed Him and attempted to kill Him for His claim to be the Son of God. Jesus handled this vicious attack on His identity with poise. He knew who He was and what He was called to do. Nothing could shake that confidence.

"What had previously seemed like random memories of Jesus' early years, actually match the first six stages of blessing"

Jesus – cursed for us

Although He was the first fully blessed person to walk the earth since Adam, there was one moment in time when Jesus was not blessed – He was cursed.

During the agonizing hours upon the cross, Father God momentarily stripped His Son of His glory and caused Him to become a curse as a form of payment for our sins (see Galatians 3:13). Jesus absorbed into His very being the curse that was due us according to God's holy laws. Not only does believing in the purpose for His death and resurrection spare us from eternal punishment after death, it also gives us the opportunity to be free from every form of curse in our own lives. As a result we have the awesome opportunity to embrace every missed blessing that God intended for us.

We bless you

We bless your personal faith in Jesus Christ. May you not only believe what He has said, but receive what He has promised for your life.

We bless your spiritual disciplines, that you will become passionately devoted to the pursuit of His purposes for your life. May your devotional life be motivated by desire and not by duty. May the written Word of God become a living Word to your soul.

We bless your walk with God, that you may become a faithful follower of Jesus Christ. May your mind be bound to His thoughts, your hands bound to His work, and your feet bound to His path for your life.

We bless your journey to wholeness. May you discover the secrets for receiving your blessings through the pattern of Jesus' life. May you bear much fruit as you continue to abide in Jesus, the vine.

Endnotes

[1] Brooks, Philip. Sherwood Eliot Wirt & Kersten Beckstrom, eds. *Living Quotations for Christians,* p.126. Harper & Row Publishers, New York. 1974.

CHAPTER EIGHT

Conception

Am I welcome in this world?

After this Elizabeth became pregnant... "The Lord has done this for me," she said. "In these days He has shown His favour."

Luke 1:24-25

Before the expectant mother knows she is pregnant, the basic relationship between mother and child is forged.

Barry Werth[1]

The manner in which you were conceived, and how the news of your conception was received, determines your initial sense of welcome into this world. The way you were welcomed in turn influences the way you relate to people for the rest of your life. We believe that the seeds of rejection are sown at conception. We also believe that later in life blessing can uproot them.

We pastored for many years before we understood or taught the power of blessing. Terry was often engaged in pastoral counselling, and on one occasion a young couple he barely knew had requested premarital counselling.

The appointment with Shayne and Julie wasn't going very well. Julie was speaking to her fiancé a little harshly and he was trying to obtain her approval. He was over-sensitive, and she didn't notice. It was awkward to watch.

As Shayne, a new believer in Christ, shared his life story, the thought suddenly dropped into Terry's mind that Shayne may have been conceived out of wedlock, and that this young man's insecurities might somehow be related to that fact. Sensing that the thought may have come from the Holy Spirit, Terry leaned toward Shayne, looked straight into his eyes and said, "Shayne, you were not an accident. You were meant to be on this earth." Instantly, the tension in the room dissolved. Shayne buried his head in Julie's shoulder and sobbed brokenly.

Shayne had indeed been a product of an unexpected pregnancy of an unmarried woman. He had also been unaccepted. The script for Shayne's identity began to be written when his mother discovered she was having the unplanned child. The words she spoke about him before his birth, and the stories she told him later, imprinted the word "accident" onto his identity. While he knew that Christ had forgiven him, he felt he did not belong. Because he failed to receive the warm welcome that everyone requires at conception, at 21 years of age Shayne still believed the lie that others rejected him. Terry's words broke that lie. At that time we didn't know what else to say to Shayne. We simply hoped Shayne and Julie would somehow learn to love each other. If we could find Shayne today, we would add words such as these:

You existed before you were born. Your life didn't begin on your "birth day," it began on your "earth day," the day you were conceived. Your spirit was placed in your mother's womb by God who prepared it in heaven. God was intimately involved on that day regardless of the circumstances of your conception. While there may be such a thing as illegitimate sex, there is no such thing as an illegitimate birth. Without heaven's permission your spirit would not have been released to earth.

The very fact that you are here today is proof that God

has a plan for your life (see Psalm 139:16). In order for you to fulfill God's plan for your life, it was essential for God to release you to the world when He did. He believed in you enough that He was sure you would make it through mountains of rejection and years of unanswered questions. He knew you would arrive at this day when all the lies are put to rest as you discover your unique and essential place in His plan. We welcome you to our world.

That's what we would like to say to Shayne, and that's what we have said to many others because those words are true.

If you have ever struggled with a sense of not belonging and a question of why you were born, or if you have sought a reason for when and where you were born, then dear one, receive the truth into the depth of your heart: Welcome! You belong here and we are excited that God brought you here at this time. It may be that even while you are reading these words, the Holy Spirit is adding words of truth to affirm and personalize this message to your heart. You deserve it.

And there's more. Once heaven gave permission for you to begin your journey to earth, your parents, especially your mother, were assigned as the gatekeepers of your tiny unprotected spirit embedded in the womb. During that time the initial formation of your body took place. Methodically, slowly, the growth process of your body made room for your emotions, mind and will to begin functioning and relating to one another. Finally you were delivered as a whole person, ready to greet the world and discover for yourself who you are and what you are called to do.

You have a purpose for being here.

Why we believe your spirit arrived at conception

You may ask how we can so confidently assert that your spirit was made alive at conception. This is a question worth exploring.

You have a soul. In simple terms, your soul is your mind, will and emotions. It's the seat of your personality.

We also know that humans are uniquely gifted with a spirit (see 1Thessalonians 5:23, and Hebrews 4:12). Through our spirit we sense the presence of God, and are able to discern God's communications. Without a spirit living within us we would not be able to have a personal relationship with God through Jesus Christ.

How does our spirit become part of us? A little deductive reasoning based on science and Scripture might help us arrive at a conclusion.

Jesus said, "flesh gives birth to flesh, and spirit gives birth to spirit" *(John 3:6),* and also, "the Spirit (of God) gives life; the flesh counts for nothing" *(John 6:63).* Therefore, we understand that a spirit is not created through the process of conception, nor is it formed along with a child's body during gestation. A person's spirit is given by God and returned to Him when the person dies (see Ecclesiastes 12:5-7).

> *"Your life didn't begin on your 'birth day', it began on your 'earth day', the day your were conceived."*

The question remains: at what point during pre-birth development is a child gifted with a spirit?

The Bible tells us, "the life of a creature is in the blood" *(Leviticus 17:11).* If the Spirit gives life, and if life is in the blood, it is reasonable to assume that at the time the circulatory system begins to function, God has already placed a spirit within that person.

Here is where science can help. It is now a scientific fact that a rudimentary circulatory system becomes active within ten days after conception – that is, before a woman would typically even know she is expecting. Therefore, before your mother even made the announcement to your father and her friends that you were on the way, your spirit had already been made alive. You were already spiritually alive and waiting to be welcomed.

Examples from Scripture

A visit with Zechariah (see Luke 1:5-25): Zechariah had just won the "Levitical lottery." When his tribe was on duty in Jerusalem, his name was drawn by lot to minister in the holy place – a once in a lifetime privilege.

While Zechariah was performing the sacred rituals alone, the angel Gabriel made a rare and unexpected appearance. He announced to Zechariah that he and his wife Elizabeth would receive the answer to their prayer of many years – Elizabeth would give birth to a son. He gave Zechariah specific details concerning the identity and destiny of their son-to-be, and told him to call him John.

Zechariah responded with unbelief. "How can I be sure that what you are saying is true?" *(Luke 1:18)*.

That is *not* what you should ask an angel who has just told you your prayers have been answered. As a result, Gabriel applied "heavenly duct tape" to Zechariah's mouth, and he couldn't talk until his son was born. Why did Gabriel silence Zechariah? Was it just to punish him?

We believe the angel struck Zechariah dumb to protect John. Words are powerful – they impart blessing or curse. By applying the angelic gag order, God prevented Zechariah from speaking wrong words about John in unbelief. If John was to be "the greatest one born of woman" (see Matthew 11:11) as Jesus claimed, then he required the greatest blessing of anyone born. In order to ensure that John would have the fullest blessing at the first crucial stage in his life, Zechariah was rendered speechless. He remained dumb until he was willing to give his first son an appropriate welcome in agreement with the angel's announcement of John's identity and destiny.

Nine months later, when it came time to name their little boy, a family discussion ensued. Sons were expected to be named after their fathers. They discussed possibilities: Zechariah Jr.; Zechariah the 2nd; maybe Zachie. A hush came over the group as Zechariah reached for the writing tablet upon which he scrawled authoritatively, "His name is John" *(Luke 1:63)*. At that instant, his voice returned and he burst forth in prophetic declaration of blessing upon his son. The blessing addressed the magnitude of God's purpose and plan for John's life. The event became widely known in the region where Zechariah and Elizabeth lived. It helped affirm John's calling in the minds of many.

Meanwhile, Gabriel also visited a teenager named Mary. To her he announced the prophesied virgin birth which was unprecedented and impossible without supernatural intervention. Nevertheless, taking the angel at his word, Mary blessed the coming miraculous conception with the words, "May it be done to me according to your word" *(Luke 1:38)*. Her response was much different than Zechariah's. She responded with faith – a remarkable response in light of the shame she would have to face once word spread that she was expecting a child before marriage.

Zechariah, Elizabeth, Joseph and Mary – they all required angelic intervention in order to welcome their unique sons properly into the world. Without this warm welcome, the identities of both children would have been questioned and possibly rejected. If John, the greatest one born of women, and Jesus, the Son of God Himself, needed a welcoming blessing into this world, how much more do we need it?

If you are reading these words, it's safe to assume that you have progressed beyond the stage of conception! Perhaps it's a little too late, you're thinking, to look for a blessing that expresses a warm welcome into the world. God can make up for it.

In one of our meetings, Henry, an aboriginal pastor, heard

this teaching and realized that his life-long sense of not belonging had to do with the shame surrounding his "earth" day. He was the unexpected product of sexual assault, and often in his early days his mother reminded him of it.

During prayer ministry one evening, a picture came to his mind of a figure doing a traditional dance and jumping with excitement, crying, "That's my son!" He immediately understood Him to be God, his Father. The experience brought lasting change. Many months later Henry explained that the sense of not belonging had all but disappeared from his life:

> Praise God for His healing and the freedom I have. I have an identity – I'm created in the image of God, a precious son called by name before I was in my mother's womb, with a destiny. Hallelujah!

Henry's parents weren't available to bless him, but he received the blessing in prayer through a personal word from God while trusted friends prayed for him.

It is, therefore, possible to make up a child's lack of welcome into the world. Words of blessing are always powerful and displace lies we might not even have recognized. Such was the case with a couple who experienced dramatic improvement in the quality of their family life through a simple act of repentance and a regular routine of speaking words of blessing. Grant and Tracy, who pastor a church in a small town, sent this wonderful testimony:

> Hearing your message on the response at conception, my wife and I were both convicted by the Holy Spirit. Our first two children were planned pregnancies. Yet, when our third child came along she was unexpected.
>
> When my wife told me the news, I was not joyful or excited. The opposite was true. My immediate response

*was along the lines of, 'Oh no!' because I hadn't want-
ed another child.*

*Although I later changed my views and looked upon
her as a gift of God, there has always seemed to be a
response in her life, 'Do I have to go to church again?
I don't want to be there!' Regardless of how much we
talked to her and prayed for her, this negative response
persisted.... Even months before we prepared to attend
a Christian camp, our daughter's consistent response
was, 'I don't want to go, do I have to?'*

*We were convicted by the Holy Spirit and repented
before God. The change in the last month has been
incredible! Our daughter now wants to be at church. She
leads in prayer, and her relationship with us is changing.*

The truth made an impact on this family. No child can
enter this world outside of God's will and without a unique
purpose.

A word of caution, however, for those who hope that
application of blessing will instantly resolve family relationships with miraculous breakthroughs or sudden
changes in behaviour. If blessing has been missing for a
long time, deep resentments may have taken root, and it
may be necessary to resolve issues first before attempting
a blessing. Also, in our experience blessing may work more
quickly when parents are in agreement and when issues
requiring repentance are first identified and addressed. It
often takes great patience to keep speaking blessing while
a formerly hardened heart slowly melts under the sweet-
ness of God's presence conveyed through the words (see
Proverbs 25:15).

As you study each stage of development and the related
blessing, remember that a blessing has more power than a
curse, and that your heavenly Father will lead you to dis-

cover the secrets for unlocking the doors to the hearts of the ones you love. While it is their choice to open the doors of their hearts, blessing (heaven's WD-40®) applied at the right time and place, lubricates the hinges on the ones that are stuck.

We bless you
We bless the day of your conception. Welcome to this world!

We bless your uniqueness. You are God's choice. Out of the hundreds of millions of possible combinations from your parents' DNA, God determined that you would be you.

We bless the timing of your arrival on earth. You were no accident. God wanted you here for this time and for His purpose and so He gave permission for your spirit to be sent to earth at exactly the right time regardless of the human circumstances.

We bless the destiny that was preplanned for your life. Before the foundation of the earth, you existed in the mind and heart of God. All the days of your life were ordained before one of them came to be (see Psalm 139:16). May you discover the sheer joy of walking in the steps that God has ordered for your life.

We bless your eternal home. The same Heavenly Father who sent your spirit to earth is waiting to welcome you back to Himself one day. May your stay on earth include a rich personal relationship with Jesus Christ while He prepares a place in heaven just for you (see John 14:2).

Endnotes

[1] Werth, Barry. *From Conception to Birth – A Life Unfolds,* p.7. Doubleday, New York. New York, 2002.

CHAPTER NINE

Pregnancy

Is there a safe place for me in this world?

*You brought me out of the womb...from my mother's
womb, You have been my God.*

Psalm 22:9.10

*It seems hard to believe that stress starts before birth.
Ultra sound images make the womb look like such a
fluid, peaceful place. In reality, children in utero seem to
be very sensitive to their mother's stress levels.*

Globe and Mail[1]

C an something that happened to you before you were
born affect your life? It did for Steve.

We met Steve and his wife Melanie when we were invited to share about the blessings of Jesus at the Bible College
where they served on staff. We taught on the blessing that
accompanies birth, and we invited people to come forward
for personal ministry. A particularly strong sense of God's
presence filled the auditorium.

Steve barely made it to the front before collapsing on the
floor where he remained sobbing until the meeting was
over. God took care of some deep wounds.

Melanie explained that Steve had been conceived out of
wedlock to a young man and woman who led the youth
group in their church. They were so ashamed that they qui-
etly went to the U.S. for an abortion, but after a weekend

of frustrated efforts, they changed their minds and returned home. They were forgiven and readily accepted by their church family. They soon married and became excited over the expected arrival.

Although Steve was eventually born to two parents who truly loved and wanted him, the pre-birth trauma plagued him all his life. He found it very difficult to share his emotions and often seemed aloof. No matter how many times his parents verbalized their love for him the word "accident" was still written into the script of Steve's life story. But that day heaven found an inroad into Steve's heart, and the Holy Spirit spoke truth to his inner being. The next day Melanie sent us an email describing the change in her husband:

Yesterday...wow! It's hard to describe what happened. All we know is that God broke that curse about his life being an 'accident' and a shameful act that had to be covered. I think my husband discovered a sense of identity and belonging in Christ that he hasn't known before. I'll tell you, from a wife's perspective, he is noticeably more at peace. I suppose that time will tell all that God did in him. We're still in the processing mode.

Time did tell. Three months later Melanie added to the story:

I can definitely say that the results have lasted. My husband is softer now. He has a greater servant's heart. His relationship with his parents is growing deeper than it has ever been, and he is consistently making time to be with them. The work that God did in my husband also seemed to give him more of a pastor's heart for the people to whom we minister. The best way to describe the lasting change is to call it 'softness' – praise God!

It is common knowledge that whatever an expectant mother permits physically into her body will be passed on in measure to her child. Research has also confirmed that the same can be true for emotions. Recently, the University of Minnesota released a study in which the author claims there is substantial evidence indicating that pre-born children readily absorb a measure of the stress, anxiety and negative emotions affecting their mother.[2] Events such as these affecting Steve's conception, should not take us by surprise when we realize that during pregnancy emotions are already emerging in the unborn child.

Think of it for a minute. If someone criticizes you, you have the mental facility to discern whether the criticism is valid. Assuming you also have the emotional maturity, you have the choice and the ability to accept or reject it. Even as adults, we sometimes allow unkind and untrue words to gain access to our heart and affect how we view ourselves and our world. What effect would those words have on us if our mind, will and emotions were still being formed in utero? With no way of knowing what to accept and what to reject, we would be totally dependent upon the protection of the one who carried us.

Fortunately we also absorb positive emotions, as we see in the example of the two pre-born boys, Jesus and John the Baptist. Blessing reached them before they were born through the interplay between their mothers – Mary and her older female relative, Elizabeth (see Luke 1:26-56).

The story of Mary and Elizabeth and their children was recorded by Dr. Luke who always had a special place for women in his writings, and probably delivered a few babies in his day. It demonstrates the importance of blessing during pregnancy while the baby is developing, beginning to feel emotions, and to wonder, *Is there a safe place for me in this world?*

Mary, a young, newly pregnant, unmarried girl, needed a blessing, and she needed it quickly. Scripture does not speak of how her own immediate family took the good news. However, it is certain that her hometown of Nazareth would have been filled with gossip about the event. Who would have believed that she was carrying the Lord of the universe within her?

But God had prepared a safe place for Mary and the unborn Jesus during her crucial first trimester – the home of her friend and extended family member Elizabeth. Before Mary and her tiny Little One could hear any negative words of shame or cursing, she hurried to visit with her older mentor.

When Elizabeth heard Mary's greeting, her own "bundle in the oven," John, leapt in her womb. They were both filled with the Holy Spirit and prophetically Elizabeth spoke a powerful blessing over Mary and her baby:

Blessed are you among women, and blessed is the child you will bear. Blessed is she who has believed that what the Lord has said to her will be accomplished! (Luke 1:42, 45)

Elizabeth was the first person in history to recognize Jesus as her Lord. She acknowledged Him as being fully God and fully man even while He was still inside His mother.

Elizabeth was favoured; Mary was blessed. Mary's famous prophetic poem of blessing, the *Magnificat,* is recorded for all of history to read and sing. She was truly a blessed woman, and all generations have called her blessed (see Luke 1:48).

Stress during pregnancy

Mary, just like many moms, was in a position for major stress during her pregnancy. Many things cause stress for moms-to-be. They might feel too young, too old, too poor, too sick – alone, fat, moody, anxious. The list goes on. Perhaps a mom is a single parent dealing with loss and grief. Perhaps she is already overwhelmed with a house full of children and sees only another mouth to feed. The baby picks up these feelings.

During pregnancy a woman and her child both need freedom from the physical and emotional stresses that impair the development of the baby. If Dad is not able or available, then others can come alongside to help create the right environment and to speak blessing into their lives.

We often encourage single moms with the insight that Scripture does not indicate the involvement of men when Jesus and John received their blessings (see Luke 1). God used two women to speak the heavenly Father's blessing prophetically into the lives of their unborn sons.

> *"God used two women to speak the heavenly Father's blessing prophetically into the lives of their unborn sons"*

In our workshops, we also teach people how to recognize the signs that they might have missed the blessing required at the time of pregnancy. Some of the common symptoms of missed blessing include persistent fear, anxiety, or guilt for no discernible reason, or a tendency to take emotional responsibility for others beyond what is reasonable or expected.

We take every opportunity to model what blessing looks like for unborn children, and often when we pray for moms, their babies move vigorously.

A woman's perspective

For the past number of years, Melissa has had an effective ministry to expectant moms. As the one in our marriage with the experience, we felt that it would be best for her to describe it in her own words.

Pregnancy! What a blessing and privilege! As a mother of three children, I can say, what an honour it is to have been a co-creator with God. I have borne three eternal souls created in His image, for His glory, because He wanted them here on earth. Thank you Lord.

I believe that pregnant women are to be honoured with special treatment – the 'red carpet' should be rolled out for them.

What is happening in their bodies for nine months is miraculous and holy. The Holy Spirit is brooding over them the way He brooded over Mary so long ago. The Lord is with them as He was with Mary. They are favoured, and have the amazing responsibility and stewardship of another life within them.

For this reason, in our ministry, I have taken a special interest in every pregnant woman I encounter. Somehow I can 'sniff' them out in a room even before they are 'showing.' I asked once where we ministered, 'Is anyone here expecting?' The woman I asked had found out that she was pregnant just that day. Like a magnet, I am drawn to them because they need a blessing.

Women in the 'middle years,' the Elizabeth years, have a special calling to bless young Marys whom God brings their way. Thus I have made it a purpose in life to bless new life from conception to birth.

I have prayed with many, many women through their nausea-filled first trimesters, through the sometimes tedious second trimester, and the uncomfortable, hope-filled third trimester, to full term. We have prayed together through labour and delivery, in good times (full-term, healthy births) and hard times (miscarriages, traumatic births, developmentally delayed babies, sin-

gle-parent pregnancies) to name a few. Each baby needs a blessing regardless of circumstances. The baby needs to feel, yes, it is a safe place, and there are people who love me and welcome me into the world.

A conference where we ministered was held in the central town of a farming community. In attendance was a young, expectant woman whose father was also present. After teaching on the nature of blessing, we spoke words of blessing to both the mother and child. Then we invited the grandfather of the child, the mother's dad, to add his words.

Tears streamed down the lined face of that farmer as he struggled to express what he desired for this child. We will never forget the loud "amens" that rang through the room as he closed with these words: "And may you be saved from having to experience the troubles that our generation went through."

Whatever those troubles may have been, the people from the community understood what he meant and those words released faith in the room. They affected everyone who knew the family. They were "weighty" and carried spiritual significance.

We believe that just as Aaron's simple words of blessing released the power of God upon the children of Israel, so those words spoken sincerely by the grandfather will positively affect the child and mother, for life.

We bless you

We bless your preborn days, when you were uniquely crafted and specifically designed for God's purpose.

We bless the formation of your body, that God performed in secret while you waited to be released to this world (see Psalm 139:13-15).

We bless your emotional life, that you may understand deep in your heart that God will always provide a safe place for you, a place of refuge on this earth from the forces that set themselves against you. May God's perfect love displace any fears in your life.

Endnotes

[1] *Globe and Mail.* September 21, 2002.
[2] *Ibid.*

CHAPTER TEN

Birth

Will my needs be met in this world?

The child's father and mother marvelled at what was said about Him. Then Simeon blessed them and said... "This child is destined...."

Luke 1:33

Before I formed you in the womb I knew you, before you were born I set you apart....

Jeremiah 1:5

"This child is destined...." What impressive words! What authority in the speaker's voice! Who was the speaker and what right did he have to make such a confident assertion to young Mary and Joseph about their Son Jesus whom he had never met?

By the time the old man Simeon spoke these words of blessing over Jesus, Joseph and Mary could hardly keep track of all the wonderful things being said about their child. What started as an untimely delivery in a stable, had transformed into the most memorable month of their lives for the best of reasons. Jesus and His earthly parents had been blessed more than anyone had anticipated. On more than one occasion, perfect strangers had spoken to them about their child's identity and God's destiny for His life. It was no longer a secret. The word was "out there" that this child had a very special future.

75

You might think, Of course there were prophetic announcements about Jesus when He was born. After all He is the Saviour of the world!

True enough. The uniqueness of Jesus is clearly demonstrated in what was said about Him at birth. No other person will ever receive words such as those spoken to Mary and Joseph. On the other hand, this story models how we are to bless any child at birth.

Bad timing or God's plan?

On the road travelling – can you imagine worse timing for a young woman to have her first child?

Back home mid-wives and family were preparing for this event, but Mary had to give birth without their help. Joseph hadn't made a reservation ahead of time, and they were stuck in a stable – probably a stone cave where the animals slept.

We have prettied up the original nativity scene considerably – fancy words like crèche; imaginary sculptures with doe-eyed donkeys smiling at the happy couple. Let's get real! This was an anxiety-filled evening for Mary.

In those days women often died during childbirth. C-sections were not an option. Lying on the straw in a dimly-lit cave, she wasn't singing the *Magnificat* during the final stages of a painful labour. And in the first moments after delivery, the joy of seeing their firstborn must have been dampened by the fact that none of the family was present to share it. We can sympathize with Mary!

Fortunately, shepherds arrived in response to an angelic announcement. Mary and Joseph must have been in shock and awe when the shepherds told them what they had seen. That likely would have mitigated the harshness of their situation considerably. Their words would have spiritually strengthened everyone present (see Luke 2:8-20).

These events all occurred in fulfillment of Old Testament

prophecy, but why had God pre-planned for them to happen this way? Evidently they ensured that the Son of God came into the world in a humble manner. But in addition, they set the stage perfectly for the needed blessings to be conveyed not only to the child, but also to benefit the young couple and the community around them.

In the biblical story, the shepherds added to the blessing by taking care of the birth announcement. According to Luke, after they had seen Jesus they told everyone what the angels had said about His identity. Thus Jesus' true identity was already being spread throughout the community.

What is the blessing needed at birth?

At birth the mind greets the world. Within minutes of delivery all five senses are operating and the billions of cells within a child's brain are processing the input.

Before a child learns its parents' language, its emotional needs for belonging and acceptance are in operation, and through experience the child learns how these needs are met. The question, *Will my needs be met?* is emerging in the newborn's first hours through the way the child is touched, held, fed and addressed verbally. Every child requires and deserves a positive experience. Thus the warm welcome that the little one received prior to birth is now reinforced through hands-on activities of the mother and father.

Why Bethlehem?

If Jesus had been born in Nazareth, Mary may have had a less traumatic delivery, but Jesus may have received the "wrong" blessing.

It is evident in later years of Jesus' life that extended family members didn't understand who He was. Many didn't accept His identity until after His resurrection. It's easy to imagine a family member picking Him up a few hours after birth and exclaiming, My doesn't He look just like His father Joseph!

Just like Mary needed to be away from her home during part of her pregnancy, perhaps God knew that she needed to be away at the time of delivery too. The angelic birth announcement might not have been as readily received in Nazareth as it was by those who weren't related to Jesus.

Today labour and delivery are also crucial times when family and friends can bring great comfort and blessing. We will never forget the support of our church family during the labour and delivery of our firstborn child.

> *"If Jesus had been born in Nazareth... (he) may have received the 'wrong' blessing"*

Twenty hours into the labour, Terry was on the phone to a friend who had promised to "pray us through." As they agreed in prayer, our son David began the last stage of his journey from darkness to light.

The comfort of prayer was so meaningful to Melissa, that for more than 20 years since then, she has felt called to commit herself to pray through labour and delivery with first time mothers. Many times we have felt the unseen hand of God helping medical personnel bring both mother and baby safely through traumatic moments. Melissa has discovered great joy in serving as an "Elizabeth" to young "Marys" through words of encouragement prompted by the Spirit, while in some cases standing by their side in the delivery room. For single moms this can be one of the greatest gifts they have ever received.

What's the story?
In our home we not only did the typical cake and candle ceremony on birthdays, we also made a habit of retelling the story of each child's birth. By the time they were pre-teens, our kids knew the details of their birth by heart and

could mouth the words as we spoke them. We kept up this tradition even when they entered university. If we were not able to be with them in person on their birthday, they would likely receive a long e-mail starting with the words, "I remember the day you were born...."

Stamped into their being is the understanding that they were chosen by us, prepared by God beforehand, welcomed when they arrived, and gifted uniquely for a life-purpose in God. They know the meaning of their names, and why we prayerfully, specifically chose their name for them. Their birth-story became a means of blessing them.

That is not the case with every child. In a Bible College in Canada we ministered to Karen, a young adult who has since become very dear to our hearts. As we taught on the blessing everyone needs at birth, she had a powerful encounter with her heavenly Father:

I had a struggle with my father not 'being there' my whole life. When I was born he was not at the hospital. As well, I'm the younger of two children. When my sister was born, my father wanted a boy. When he found out she was a girl, my grandfather told my father that he had better have a boy next time. So when I was born, my grandfather cursed my father for having a girl. I know that affected my dad until today.

I knew the story, but didn't know how it affected me spiritually. But when you were teaching on conception and birth, you talked about feelings: of being a burden, of having friends but never feeling like you belonged, of trying hard to please people, of being afraid of failure...it was totally me. I've always had...strong Christian friends. The church loved me, I had mentors, but I didn't know the root of my problem, or why I felt the way I did. My mom told me that I would 'grow out of it.'

She could never understand why my spirit was so down.

But then when you asked us to stand...I stood and wept.... You said, 'I want you to think about the day of your birth, but imagine Jesus there and what He would have said.' I was blown away. I have never in my life heard God's voice so clearly in my heart. He said, 'I wanted a girl!' After that I felt totally at peace.

I knew what I had to do, so I talked to my dad and forgave him...without blaming him. He hasn't replied yet, but that's okay; God's in control now.

That was only the beginning for Karen. Her new sense of self acceptance became a testimony that affected other students. She developed a burden for rejected children and found herself in Eastern Europe working with children from dysfunctional families. To her astonishment, after she returned from one of her trips, rather than her mom meeting her at the airport, her dad was there to greet her. As he drove her home he told her that he was very proud of her and that he had always loved her but hadn't known how to express it.

Karen's world has changed. The script by which she lives has been re-written through blessing. It all began with the revelation that God wanted her to be who she is. Through His Spirit, Karen's heavenly Father brought truth into the very core of her being. And because Karen was willing to forgive, she also received the long-awaited blessing from her father.

Why is ceremony important?

Blessings at birth can be imparted by others beyond members of the immediate family. When a child is born, he or she is to be officially welcomed into the community of faith and placed under the umbrella of God's protection through the prayers of those in spiritual authority.

About a month after the birth of their son, Mary and Joseph returned with Jesus, and probably several family members, to the temple in Jerusalem to observe the mandatory dedication ceremony carried out by priests (see Luke 2:21-40).

Once again God brought people, unrelated to the family, alongside them just when they needed a blessing.

God had spent years preparing two senior saints to speak with insight from the Lord concerning Jesus' identity and destiny – something Mary, Joseph, or the priests apparently would not have been able to do on their own. Simeon was "moved by the Spirit" to be at the right place at the right time. Gently picking up the baby in his arms, he announced Jesus' destiny and blessed Mary and Joseph, encouraging them in their new role as parents.

Then a venerated intercessor, an old saint who had spent her life serving God through prayer in the temple, stepped forward and revealed what God had spoken to her about this child. Anna completed the blessing that the Father in heaven had prepared for His only Son at birth.

The ceremonial dedication of Jesus enabled three generations of persons to give Him a powerful public blessing: Mary the young mother; the middle-aged family relative Elizabeth; and Simeon and Anna, the senior saints.

How does ceremony work today?

A dedication ceremony ought to be more than a ritual. God intends for it to have spiritual impact upon the child and the family.

The welcoming of a new child into the community of faith is a joint celebration between heaven and earth. It's a time when God can empower the family with treasures from His storehouse to equip them to guide their child into his or her destiny.

Knowing the power of blessing in our own lives, we made a *big* deal out of baby dedications in our church.

Whether your church practices infant baptism or a dedication ceremony, imparting blessing is the order of the day.

We invite both sets of grandparents, relatives, god-parents, and friends whom the parents choose, to stand alongside the family. We urge parents to choose a life-Scripture that they publicly proclaim over their child. We announce the meaning of the child's name, and invoke special prayers that include time for seeking the guidance of the Holy Spirit concerning the child's destiny. Sometimes God speaks about the child's future (prophetic words). We share these thoughts with the parents, encourage parents to record them, and allow the words to be tested over time.

What? God speaks? And now, we feel we need to address a question we can almost hear some of you asking: Speaks to us? What do you mean God speaks to us? That sounds way out to me!

Actually it's Scriptural. We believe God talks to people today. Here's why and how.

Jesus declared that the Holy Spirit speaks (see John, 16:3) to every one who believes in Him, and offers them guidance. He said that the heavenly Father comes and makes a home in the hearts (see John 14:23) of those who love Him.

Thus everyone who is a child of God through Jesus has the privilege of hearing the voice of God through the Holy Spirit. As God's child, hearing His voice is your birthright.

We like to say that the only father who doesn't speak to his children is one who is angry, or one who is far away. Your heavenly Father is neither. Your heart is His home and He doesn't want to give you the silent treatment.

How does God speak to us? Usually through our own thoughts. Distinguishing between the Spirit's voice and other thoughts that fill our minds is an acquired skill, but as we renew our minds with truth and submit our wills to His desires, we learn the delight of recognizing the voice of the Spirit within us. Not only does this help us recover missed blessings, but obeying God-given inner promptings is also key to releasing words of blessing to others in the right way at the right time.

The power of dedication: Interesting things happen during baby dedication ceremonies.

During one particularly large ceremony, family and friends of the parents lined the front of the sanctuary from one side to the other. As we shared the truth that God authors, and desires the birth and life of every child who is conceived, a first-time visitor, then a single mother, later reported gaining profound insight as a result:

> I was raised in a Christian home, but had been away from both God and church for more than ten years. I found myself in a new town, unemployed, alone and pregnant with my third child. Feeling desperate, I attended a morning service while a baby was being dedicated. I couldn't help feeling so alone and full of shame.
>
> Pastor Terry, whom I had never met, said that God had just put something on his heart to share. He said that God wanted somebody to know that every child is a gift from Him, and that no matter what the circumstance, each child was created for a reason. I knew that was meant for me, and felt instantly touched by God's love. God opened my eyes to see how much He loved me and my children.
>
> God has now placed my family in a cell group led by the parents of the baby that was dedicated at that first morning service where God spoke to me.

It was thrilling to see a single mother find new friends and learn to bless her own child by watching the blessing and dedication of another couple's baby.

In another instance, a local pastor shared the story of his own dedication as a baby to encourage us and demonstrate that Spirit-led words of blessing at the time of a child's dedication are a powerful influence in shaping a child's life.

I am the oldest of six children, wrote Steve. My parents met as single missionaries in Malawi, Africa. Shortly after my brother was born, our parents decided to dedicate us as part of the African church tradition. I know that my parents did not understand the power of blessing as we do now. Neither would they have believed at that time in the gift of prophecy, but they did love God and were led by the Spirit as they knew how. As part of our dedication, they blessed us both to become full-time Christian workers.

They never told this to me or my brother as we were growing up. In fact, whatever career we talked about, they endorsed. My brother and I however, both pursued Bible college training and we both became pastors. It was only then that our parents told us of the blessing they had prayed over us.

Of interest to me is that my parents did not pray a similar blessing over any of our other siblings and while most are active followers of Jesus, only my brother and I are in full-time ministry.

We had a similar experience with our third child Mark. A woman in our church at the time gave us a life-shaping Scripture for Mark when he was born. Along with the Scripture, she shared what she felt the Holy Spirit was saying about our boy's future. We pondered her words, and like Mary, treasured them, holding them close to our hearts for more than a dozen years.

One day when our son was 13, he felt God speak something similar to his heart. Only then did we share those words with him. Today we have already seen some of those words come to pass, and we are able to help Mark plan for the special future that we have pictured with him.

What's in a name?

Your child's name is part of his/her blessing at birth. Names are inextricably bound to a person's identity. If someone wants to know who you are, they ask your name. Bible names were generally assigned for their meaning and purpose. For example, Joseph had the right and responsibility to name Mary's son. He followed the angel's instructions to name Him Jesus – meaning, The Lord Saves. A name was officially conferred on a child at circumcision. From the day of Jesus' circumcision onward, every time someone spoke His name, they prophesied His future.

The name you have been given may not seem as profound, yet we are constantly surprised how God brings blessing upon children through their names. More on names in Chapter 14.

We bless you

We bless the day of your birth. May you know that your needs will always be met according to the supply of the One who sent you to this earth to accomplish His purpose through you.

We bless your gender, for you were created to be a man or a woman, according to God's design.

We bless your birth order, in the family to which you were given. May the timing of your arrival and the relationships with family members be used by God to perfect you according to His will.

We bless your mental growth, as you begin to process the world around you. May your ear gates and eye gates be guarded by those who care for you and keep you in their home.

We bless your spiritual journey. May it begin with a dedication to a faith community that follows Jesus Christ. May you be guarded and guided by human and angelic beings until you are old enough to make your own choices.

CHAPTER ELEVEN

Early Childhood

Who can I trust in this world?

People were bringing little children to Jesus to have Him touch them... and He took the children in His arms, put His hands on them and blessed them.

Mark 10:13a, 16

Little children have BIG feelings.

Anonymous

A friend of ours was praising his pre-teen for some little accomplishment when his mother, who happened to be visiting at the time, interrupted him to say, "You compliment your children too much – you're going to make them proud."

Perplexed, he told us the story of how harsh his own childhood had been. Unfortunately his, like so many other childhoods we have heard about, was characterized by a combination of lack of affection and abundance of correction.

Where did we get the misconception that character in little people is built through constant correction? Do we really expect that expressing adult-sized anger toward tiny tots will produce godly character? Early childhood ought to feel more like a recreational summer camp than a military boot camp.

Yes, discipline is essential, and we will address it, but let's understand that a parent's first role in a child's life is to provide and protect, not punish and correct.

Kind words nourish little souls like plant food on tender shoots. Critical words bend and even break them.

A wise man once said, "as the twig is bent, so grows the tree." We have seen far too many "bent twigs" grow up to be bent-right-out-of-shape "trees." In fact, the way some people dishonour children makes us downright angry. We are in good company on that score, for even Jesus became angry about the treatment of little lives He desired to bless.

Parents, and others, brought children (Scripture says, "little" children) to Jesus in order for Him to bless them – they believed that God's favour would be upon every little life that received loving words and a meaningful touch from the Master's hands.

These children were not infants. They likely ranged from toddler to pre-teen, because the wording for "little ones" in the original language refers to young children (*paidion* in Greek), not babies. Most were at that marvellous stage of life where trust comes naturally and social graces have not yet been learned. It's easy to picture Jesus picking one of them up to pray for them, while the others clamour about Him crying, Me too!

The disciples criticized the people for bothering Jesus with little children. You can almost hear them saying, Take that kid out of here! She's getting in the way! Don't you know that the Master is preparing to give an important message from God?

Yes, He was about to give an important message from God – to the disciples. In Mark's Gospel it says that Jesus became "indignant," that is angry, over injustice. Jesus looked the disciples square in the face and rebuked the rebukers saying, "Let the little children come to me and do not hinder them" *(Mark 10:13-16)*. The words had impact. Jesus made it plain that a person's value is not determined by their age or abilities. The blessing He gave them imparted spiritual life, invited God's favour, and set an example for parents to follow.

Jesus – blessed as a toddler

The familiar story of the visit from the Wise Men refers to Jesus being blessed at the toddler stage in life. The traditional story doesn't always line up with Scripture. Unlike the version on standard Christmas cards, the three kings didn't arrive together on a one-humped camel that snuck into the manger on the night of Jesus' birth!

The *Magi,* men from a land to the east, had seen a sign in the heavens that they interpreted as an indication of the birth of a king (see Matthew 2). When they arrived in Jerusalem they sought and found "the young child." The word used here in reference to Jesus is the same word used in reference to the children Jesus blessed (see Mark 10). The Saviour of mankind was no older than preschool age when the *Magi* blessed Him, yet these important men gave Him honour reserved for a king. They were not embarrassed to kneel before Him and worship Him.

Dishonour in early childhood

God intends for every child to be honoured. Unfortunately, that doesn't always happen.

Little people have big feelings. And when their value is discounted by adults, the dishonour that results blocks blessing. Without a blessing children do not learn to trust others and grow in grace as did Jesus during His early childhood (see Luke 2:40). Parents dishonour their children in many ways.

Improper Punishment: Quoting from his book, *The Strong-Willed Child,* Dr. James Dobson said on a radio program that a child's will emerges in the first year of his/her life and dominates by the second year.

What word do very young children hear more than any

other from their parents? *"No!"* Don't touch this; don't do that; and so on. Somewhere during the second year of a child's life they discover that the umbilical cord has been cut and that they are an independent entity that can walk anywhere they choose and put anything in their mouth light enough to pick up with their own hands.

They are experimenting with their new-found physical freedom without the benefit of any life experience – certainly a recipe for disaster if left unchecked.

The challenge for a parent, as Dr. Dobson says, is "to shape the will without breaking the spirit." Parents need to apply wise and balanced "love and limits" to bring proper correction without damaging a tender young personality.

The Bible says, "Folly is bound up in the heart of a child, but...discipline will drive it far from him" *(Proverbs 22:15).*

Folly, an inborn nature, believes, If I get my own way all the time, I will be happy. Left unchecked, that folly manifests itself through an untamed will. We all have it to one degree or another. Training that untamed will requires parental discipline.

Children become "bent out of shape" when parents mistake punishment for discipline. Punishment is pain administered as a form of payment for wrongdoing, whether physical, or in the form of temporary denial of privileges. Discipline, on the other hand, is the training of the untamed will to make godly choices.

Punishment disciplines a child only when it is administered fairly (i.e. if the punishment fits the crime), consistently, without anger, and never before the child has been warned. When punishment is not administered fairly, it sends confusing or hurtful messages to a child such as, rules are more important than relationship, and the child's opinion doesn't count. Children who have been punished unfairly often harbour deep resentment that remains buried until it bursts forth later in life.

The application of godly discipline must be tailored to each child. Each child's individuality must be recognized and nurtured. You must discover what motivates the child before you can assist in training their will. The goal of parental discipline is to bring children to the place where they have enough inner motivation to make good choices on their own.

"as the twig is bent, so grows the tree"

Parents often use compliance as a measuring stick – a compliant child is deemed obedient and therefore does not appear to require punishment or discipline. While compliant children make their parents proud because they obey readily, eventually as they grow they may also have a tendency to follow the wrong crowd. Strong-willed children are often harder to handle as pre-schoolers because they don't follow instructions as easily. They may lead the wrong crowd later on, but they will never *follow* it!

Another form of improper punishment is neglect. The old saying that two wrongs don't make a right, is applicable. Not to discipline a child properly is to devalue them as a person.

Sexual experiences: Who can I trust? asks the young child. A child's trust in the early years can be decimated by sexual abuse.

Sexual abuse is one of the greatest breaches of trust that a child can experience. It not only blocks blessing, it curses a child's sense of identity, and is, unfortunately, far more common than we want to admit. If you were sexually abused as a child, then please understand that the child victim of an adult aggressor is never at fault. You did nothing to deserve such dishonour. But you must do something about the wound. Time on its own does not heal this kind of wound. Our advice to you is this: start the process of rebuilding trust by speaking with a qualified professional who shares your spiritual values.

School experiences: Teachers are tremendously influential in shaping children's self worth at the elementary school level. Most of us can remember a moment of shame or embarrassment at the hands of an insensitive teacher.

Rosalie Pedder teaches teachers. She has traveled to dozens of countries for Youth With a Mission (YWAM) training leaders how to teach their students, and she has observed potential effects of a negative classroom environment on little hearts and minds:

> *I am constantly amazed by how many of our students and staff have suffered some form of abuse at school. Words have tremendous power, and as Proverbs 18:21 says, they have the power of life and death. ...Offences against students... take the form of sarcasm, humiliation... ignoring them or regularly sending them out of the room. It shows up when teachers force students to do things their way, not allowing for any individuality.[1]*

On the other hand, a teacher who believes in a student and recognizes their gifting can instil worth and value when it is missing in a child's life. A man at one of our workshops testified that he was never affirmed in his family and was subject to much criticism at a young age. However, one of his school teachers believed in him and made a habit of speaking encouragement into his life in such a way that this man began to believe in his own potential. Today he credits the teacher for single-handedly bestowing on him blessing that was so lacking in his life. God bless teachers who bless!

Accidental injury: Regarding childhood experiences, people can be reluctant to open their hearts to the Lord for His examination. "My parents loved me and did the best they knew how," is a common response. People understandably battle a feeling of disloyalty to their parents when they discuss events that hurt them while growing up. But to say that you sustained a wound along the way is not necessarily the same as blaming your parents.

Sometimes the worst injuries are the ones that happen accidentally. Ice hockey, for example, is known to be a rough sport – body contact is permitted and encouraged. When Terry played, no one feared his body checks because they didn't hurt. But on one occasion Terry accidentally fell onto another player while chasing a loose puck. The poor fellow had to be carried off the ice on a stretcher and he didn't walk again for six weeks. Accidents happen, and they hurt.

Accidental emotional injury happens too, and it hurts. Not only that, it can block blessing from reaching a young child in the same way as a deliberate curse. At a missionary conference where Terry was speaking, a couple in leadership sought personal counsel for this very reason.

They were deemed successful and were well liked, yet all the time the wife Brenda suffered silently. She had heard from her mother many times throughout her early childhood how painful she had been to deliver at birth. "See – you're the cause of all my pain," the mother had often said in jest, thinking Brenda understood that she was being teased. But Brenda took it seriously. She harboured the lie and carried it into adulthood where it "bent" her relationship patterns. She relates:

I have walked with the Lord for 30 years, and from the first day I was convinced of God's amazing love for His children. However, I struggled to believe that He loved me. Inwardly I suffered with a spirit of rejection. I had two loving parents, a great family and good friends, yet I couldn't break free from self-condemnation and self-hatred. I could never... go for ministry because my feelings seemed to have no basis or legitimacy.

When my husband and I heard you speak at the conference, I was desperate. I wanted to be free from the weight...on my heart. After the family blessing teaching, I thought and prayed about my conception and delivery. I knew that I had been a 'surprise' for my parents and had had a traumatic birth that caused my mother much pain.

The Lord revealed a number of issues...and showed Himself in each step of my life from the very beginning. Something was supernaturally unlocked for me. Since that time I have experienced an ability to accept myself (both strengths and weaknesses), I have less fear of people, and a new understanding of God's limitless love for me. ...My ministry on the mission field has been enhanced and my relationships are deeper.

Later that year some of Brenda's friends told us that they had noticed a positive and lasting change in her.

Neglect of playtime: Playtime with the kids is more important than we assume. Imaginary tea parties, doll houses and wrestling matches have their place in imparting blessing to young children.

When we met Rev. Mark Hill, he was a Sociology Ph.D. candidate doing research on fatherlessness in certain cultures.

According to his research, both medical and sociological, our brains grow approximately one trillion cells during the first 12 years. During play the brains of young children are growing. Distinctions are visible in brain scans of those who do, and do not receive adequate stimulation through play. Mark Hill believes a father's prime role during pre-school years is to play with his children. As a sociologist he claims that the lack of adequate playtime has a profound impact on children for the rest of their lives.

Mothers as well as fathers can "hinder little children" from coming into the blessing of Jesus when they fail to recognize their child's need for parental involvement in play. At the very least, a willingness to get down to their level and interact with young children communicates value and worth.

Children who are dishonoured in any of these ways may appear to be unaffected on the outside for a period of time, but on the inside they are affected deeply. They become prone to making false conclusions about life, and these lead them into making harmful vows.

Breaking a harmful vow

Vows are like valves. Our home has valves on the water pipes that enable us to close off the water supply to a portion of the house temporarily while a leaky faucet is being fixed. No matter how great the water supply, you don't get the flow back until the valve is reopened.

Similarly, vows regulate the flow of emotions in a person's heart. Vows can be helpful or harmful, depending on whether they are used to open or close our heart. A marriage vow is helpful because it serves as a constant reminder to open our heart to our spouse in times when there's barely a trickle of love flowing.

However, once children are old enough to discover and use willpower to get what they want, they can also use willpower to compensate for emotional injury.

That's a vow. In an attempt to avoid more hurt, they make a vow with an act of their will. Blessing cannot flow to the part of the heart that is being protected by a vow. The same act that shuts out hurt, also keeps out love.

For example, let's say that dad promises to take his son Brent fishing on Saturday. Brent counts the days, daydreaming about the big fish that will be his. Saturday morning comes and Brent is sitting on the front step waiting. Dad walks by with his briefcase on the way to a meeting he had forgotten about when he promised the fishing expedition. He tries to cover his mistake with a promise of an "even better trip" next week. But next week dad is out of town and by next month he has forgotten his promise. The fishing trip never happens. Through this event Brent begins to believe a lie – perhaps that he is not worth much, or that adults cannot be trusted. He may decide he will "never trust an adult again." The result is a closed door to part of Brent's heart.

A child can make other similar vows:

- "I will never let anyone love me."
- "I will never share what is mine."
- "I will never let anyone know I am hurt."
- "I will never allow anyone to touch me."

Many other statements can become vows as well, but they all have the same effect. Time does not heal a vow even when it has been temporarily forgotten. A vow must be recognized and renounced. When that happens, the lie associated with the vow can be instantly replaced with truth.

> *"sometimes the worst injuries are the ones that happen accidentally"*

A woman in one of our workshops realized that as a young child she had in anger made a vow that she would never marry or have children. From then on she dressed and acted in a manner that reflected her unwillingness to consider herself eligible for a love relationship with a man. The ministry team assisted her to renounce the vow and blessed her identity as a woman. Her heart immediately opened to the desire of meeting the man whom God had chosen for her. The next week she wrote a prayer for a husband which is now part of her regular devotional life.

How to bless children
What are the ingredients of spiritual food that nourishes little ones as they grow?

96

Beginning with the toddler stage, and continuing to adulthood, we impart blessing to children through intentional words, deeds and ceremonies that communicate worth and value. Gary Smalley and John Trent give an excellent summary of how to bless children in their book *The Blessing*. They list five elements of blessing:

- A meaningful touch
- A spoken message
- Attaching a high value
- Picturing a special future
- An active commitment

We have used these as a guideline to formulate blessings for people at any age and stage of life with tremendous results.

A practical application

A few unhurried minutes spent with a child one-on-one just before bed time – perhaps the most teachable time in their day – can have a huge impact. A bed time story and a little talk about how special the child is to mom and dad, followed by a hug and a prayer, may take two minutes, but it gives the gift of meaningful touch and a spoken message, and it communicates a high value on the relationship.

Consistency is demonstrated in active commitment. Rolf Garborg relates that his daughter Lisa had become so attached to the blessing he spoke over her each night, that before he left on business trips, she insisted he speak the blessing over her once for each day he would be away. Today Lisa serves God and blesses her children on a regular basis.

We helped our children picture a special future by praying with them about their future spouses when they were still preteens. Terry talked to our daughter Jessica about the special man she hadn't yet met, but whom God was even then preparing for her. Melissa told the boys how one day they would meet the girl that God had picked out just for them. We constantly spoke of the good things that God prepares for those who obey Him.

This blessing allowed our children's imaginations to be guided by the Holy Spirit. It gave them permission to dream great dreams for their lives.

Nothing is impossible for someone whose imagination is inspired by God.

We bless you

We bless your early childhood, that you may learn to trust everyone who exercises godly authority in your life.

We bless your play times, that your mind may learn and grow to your full potential. May you be kept safe at all times.

We bless your mental development, that nothing would hinder the growth of your mind to its full potential.

We bless the development of your will, that you may be shaped in wisdom and love by those in authority in your life. May you learn to make wise choices in every life-decision.

We bless your spiritual life, that you would understand and experience what it means to walk with God at a young age.

We bless your family relationships, that you would discover and enjoy a sense of belonging in a family that loves you. May you be kept safe from accidental and emotional injury and improper discipline.

We bless your school experiences. May school be a safe place for you to learn and grow. May school authorities recognize and encourage your gifts and talents.

We bless your friendships. May you may be guided to make wise choices in every relationship outside your family circle.

Endnotes

[1] Pedder Rosalie. Starting Well – *A Teacher's Guide to Sowing Seeds in Prepared Ground.* (Unpublished manuscript.)

CHAPTER TWELVE

Teen Years

Do I have what it takes?

And Jesus kept increasing in wisdom and stature and in favour with God and men.

Luke 2:52

My Father gave me the greatest gift anyone could give another person: he believed in me.

Jim Valvano[1]

"You can do it!" Our son Mark was coursing up a long, steep ski hill for the second time in a regional cross-country race.

"You're looking strong! Keep it up!" Terry could see that Mark was not yet winded. As he rounded the top, dad ran beside him for a few yards. "Now's the time to make your move. See you at the finish line!"

From the beginning of the race Terry had been positioning himself at points along the way shouting words of affirmation and encouragement. He had run that exact route thirty years before and remembered it well. After taking a shortcut down the hill, Dad hopped a fence and waited for his son on the track as he ran the last few yards.

"Great finish! Amazing run!"

Running against boys up to two years older than him, Mark had still managed to finish in the top 60 out of a field of 400 runners. Although this invitational didn't count toward school rankings, the race certainly counted in the young man's heart. He began to believe that he really did have what it takes.

Before the race Mark had a different opinion. With an exceptional athlete as a running mate, and being prone to self-criticism, Mark had developed an inaccurate view of his own abilities. He felt he could never measure up. Around the kitchen table, we couldn't talk our son out of this misconception. Terry decided to try to "be there," and shout words of affirmation at key moments during an actual race. It worked.

Mark's race is a metaphor for adolescence. It's so easy for young minds and hearts to receive the wrong message during this crucial stage of development.

At puberty, a young person's body suddenly begins to mature. This physical process helps to trigger a crucial question of the heart: *Do I have what it takes to make it in an adult world?*

Regardless of how quickly a teen matures physically, this question must receive a positive answer before a young person's heart can fully embrace their emerging adult identity. This is the time when they are most vulnerable. This is the time when affirmation is a huge need in their lives.

Arrows in the hands of a warrior

At this stage the leading role for imparting the required blessing shifts from mother to father. To understand what we mean, picture a bow and arrow. The Bible says, "Like arrows in the hand of a warrior, so are the children of one's youth" *(Psalm 127 NASB)*.

Arrows have a purpose. Each one is designed for a warrior to pick up, place in a bow, and propel to its destination.

Children, like mere sticks in a warrior's hands, require shaping. For a while they are protected in a quiver, but there comes a time when they must be taken from their safe place, loaded into a bow, aimed, and fired at God's destination for their lives. Puberty is that time.

Fathers have spiritual authority to call forth their sons and daughters from childhood into maturity. We like to say that a mother is called to string the bow and a father to shoot the arrow. But to shoot an arrow, it first has to be aimed.

The shift in spritual roles of mothers and fathers during the teen years needs to be accompanied by a shift in their parenting approach from teacher to coach. Teachers teach in an enclosed environment and exert control over every aspect of a student's behaviour. Coaches stand on the sidelines while players play the game. Coaches encourage and correct, but they can't play the game for their team.

Parents, but especially mothers, can have a difficult time adjusting to this shift in roles. The underlying assumption is that parents understand God's agenda for their teen – something that isn't always obvious. Learning to let our children learn for themselves while still giving them guidance along the way is an acquired talent.

A teen at the temple

Even Mary, Jesus' mother, had to make adjustments in her life.

When Jesus was almost 13 He and Mary exchanged words publicly that revealed her struggle with recognizing her Son's development at times (see Luke 2:41-52). The account in Luke offers excellent insight into the dynamics of parent/teen interaction.

Jesus' family was once again on the way to Jerusalem for the biggest national celebration of the year – Passover. The event doubled as a family vacation for many. On the long, three-day walk from Nazareth, they would have been joined by friends and family who they perhaps might not have seen since the previous Passover. After they reached their lodgings in Jerusalem, we can imagine Mary saying to Jesus, "Just play with your cousins, and let us know tomorrow which family you're staying with."

The days in Jerusalem would have been filled with familiar and traditional activities, just like every year. But this year Mary and Joseph failed to notice an important difference – Jesus had started to grow "peach fuzz." A subtle shift was taking place not only in His body, but also in His mind. With the need to prepare for His destiny pre-occupying His mind, Jesus stayed behind to join the temple court debates.

Experimentation mistaken for rebellion

When Mary and Joseph left the festival, they assumed Jesus was in the company of relatives, and didn't miss Him. Three days later they discovered Him sitting in the middle of a circle of rabbis answering questions with such insight that everyone listening was amazed – everyone except Mary and Joseph. They were not interested in His Scriptural knowledge at that moment. Jesus had acted uncharacteristically without parental consent, and they were more than a little perturbed.

Mary, like any other mother, had been mulling over all the possible scenarios for Jesus' disappearance while trying to hold back fear for His safety. Now that she and Joseph had found Him, their fear gave way to anger for giving them such a fright, and perhaps for spoiling the family's plans.

We have no idea of whether Jesus had made any attempt to get word to His mother that He was staying behind for a few days in the temple, however we do know that He had to do what He was doing. He was preparing for His destiny.

Unfortunately, the *urgent* took precedence over the *important* for Joseph and Mary, so Mary interrupted the Bible class abruptly with the question, "Son, why have you treated us like this?"

Without waiting until they were alone, Mary scolded Jesus in public. Because Mary and Joseph failed to recognize that their Son was engaged in important preparation for His life's calling, He received public criticism instead of public affirmation. It would have been much better for Mary to affirm His gift in public and deal with the misunderstanding in private.

Jesus' interaction with His parents in this illustration demonstrates what many teens know – that teens often first receive recognition for their gifts and talents outside their family circle. The answer to the question, *Do I have what it takes?* requires affirmation that is too often absent in a teen's own home.

Lessons from adolescent children

Teenagers long for adults to listen to them without judging them. It is a form of honour.

When Mary said, "Your father and I...," Jesus turned His attention from the rabbis and reminded Mary who His real Father was.

Rather than debate His actions, Jesus addressed the core of the misunderstanding. Mary listened to her son, and like she had done years before, "treasured all these things in her heart" *(Luke 2:51)*.

The ending to this parent/teen episode comes as no surprise. Jesus submitted to His parents even though they didn't give Him what He required at the moment. As a result, mom, step-dad and son launched out together on the long walk home with plenty of time to straighten it all out.

In a family of today, things could have turned ugly. When teens respond to dishonour with rebellion they remove themselves from the possibility of being blessed, and the devil's trap is sprung in their lives. Often that is when life-long addictions or destructive habits can take root. Anger at being dishonoured weakens self control, and young people often choose harmful substitutes for the sense of well-being that they are missing. Their identities become cursed and their destinies clouded until something removes the lies from their hearts.

Blessing brings balance

The blessing that Jesus received as a result of His obedience to His parents manifested in His life in four ways: He grew in wisdom, stature, favour with God, and favour with people (see Luke 2:52).

His development reflected perfectly balanced growth in the four areas of life: mental, physical, spiritual and social. When a person feels blessed in all these areas, their self-worth is strong, and they are less likely to acquire addictive habits or compulsive behaviour patterns. Ultimately parents don't bless a child when they sacrifice one area of development in order to promote another.

When a father fails to "pick up the arrow"

Back to the story about Jesus in the temple for a moment.

It is recorded in Luke that both parents found Jesus, but Mary did all the talking. There is no record of Joseph entering into this conversation. We don't know what he was doing while Mary was publicly confronting their boy, but it appears as if Mary did the talking for the two of them.

We have noticed that fathers often become inexplicably passive when it comes to interaction with their teens. Mothers too often have to take the initiative to discipline or interact with their teens without adequate assistance from their mate. Fathers block the blessing in their home through neglect of their teens.

Neglect: Jane tells a story of the consequences of neglect at a fragile time in her life. The Lord Himself imparted the missed blessing to her during ministry time in one of our Blessings Workshops:

I was the youngest of five children in a very authoritarian home. I always wondered why I had fond memories of my father up to grade six, and why after that everything in my life seemed to go wrong for about the next eight years (including a teen pregnancy).

When we were praying about my lack of blessing at puberty, immediately I remembered a time when I was really proud to be one of the only girls in seventh grade to qualify for the school gymnastics team. Most team members were two or three years older. We had a special assembly one evening so our parents could attend. I remembered being on the trampoline warming up and looking into the stands to see an empty seat beside my mother. Dad couldn't take the time to come see me. He sat at home in his rocking chair that evening. That hurt.

I felt unworthy and not valued. As we prayed, I realized that it was immediately after that disappointment that I dropped out of swim team, cross country and just about every other sport I truly loved. That was the moment rebellion entered my life and now I understand why I always felt I became a totally different person in seventh grade.

As I prayed with my eyes closed remembering this scene, I asked the Lord to show me where He was in all of this. In my mind's eye I was startled to see Jesus standing at the foot of the trampoline in a white robe with His hands up spotting me and a huge smile on His face. I was overwhelmed with a feeling of love and value. The Lord is so awesome. To top it off, this breakthrough came on the same day that I had volunteered to coach a girls' volleyball team for seventh and eighth graders! I am so amazed at His faithfulness.

Jane's life took a sudden turn for the worse when she was

dishonoured through neglect. Jane's father had abdicated his role at the most critical time in his daughter's life. At the very moment she required affirmation, the devil's trap was sprung in her life because she returned rebellion for dishonour.

Jane suffered the consequences of her own rebellion for a number of years and cursed her own self worth as she willingly participated in destructive behaviour. For many years there was no one to pick up the fallen arrow until Jesus Himself brought the breakthrough for Jane.

Since every breakthrough requires a follow-through, after Jane received new spiritual insight, we encouraged her close friends to seal the blessing by continuing to support her and to speak encouragement into her life.

Criticism: Jane's tragic struggle was the product of mere neglect. However, many children have to battle a more deliberate foe to their identity – constant criticism.

> "The answer to the question 'Do I have what it takes?' requires affirmation that is too often missing in the teen's own home"

Ironically, criticism is usually given in the name of encouragement. Parents think their words of correction are encouraging better performance.

We are reminded of the father who responded to his daughter's 97 percent average in school with the question, "Where are the other three marks?" He presumed that 100 percent would bring exceptional opportunities for scholarships. However what the father meant, and what the daughter heard, were virtual opposites. She received the message that even her best efforts weren't good enough. This father had more than criticized his daughter – he crushed her motivation. His words opened her heart to an act of rebellion that detoured her journey away from her God-given destiny for many years.

Thus, *correction without affirmation curses, and does not bless.* Without affirmation, correction seems like rejection and can only be overcome by repeated words of affirmation.

What about single moms?

Since the father's role is so vital for imparting the blessing at puberty, what's a single mom to do? We can hear some single moms sighing in despair as they consider the monumental task of trying to walk with their sons and daughters through the teen years without a father in sight.

It's not fair! God didn't intend for you to do this without the help of a male mentor in your children's lives. On your behalf, we pray in the pattern of Malachi 4:5-6 that God will send someone to turn the hearts of the fathers to the children, and the children to their fathers.

In the meantime, we counsel you to do whatever it takes to bring your children under positive godly influences from male role models, especially during the critical teen years. One way is through sponsoring a blessing ceremony for your child in which selected male adults are involved (see Chapter 16).

A Christian *bar mitzvah*

The Jewish culture understands the importance of ceremony to mark every important transition in life. The ancient rite of passage called *bar mitzvah* (for boys) and *bat mitzvah* (for girls) is a key element in the maturation of every orthodox Jewish child. These are no small ceremonies – they can be as sophisticated and expensive as a wedding. Some parents emulate the Jewish tradition with an elaborate Christian ceremony that has similar elements (see Chapter 16).

Even simple ceremonies and traditions can effectively

impart a sense of value and worth.

A valued tradition in our home was the father-daughter "date" that spanned Jessica's entire school age years. These were special, and often formal occasions, when Terry modeled how a man should treat a woman. He finished each date with the words, "Don't give your heart away until you meet a man who treats you this well."

Birthday parties can be used to impart blessing. When our eldest son turned 16, he needed a self-esteem boost. We planned a surprise party for him and invited youth and adults who had played a significant role in his life. After the typical festivities we invited people to take a few minutes to share out loud what they valued about David and why he was special to them. Innovation is certainly encouraged as long as it effectively communicates at least some of the five elements of blessing (see Chapter 11).

When blessing doesn't seem to work

Regardless of how diligently parents communicate worth and value to their children, or how well they communicate blessing, it is still possible for children to rebel.

A teenager we know well went through rebellion in her mid-teens against God and the values she had been taught as a child.

During this time her mother felt forewarned by the Holy Spirit to hold the line and not overreact. The mother and father were not aware of everything their daughter did, however, they could easily tell their daughter had temporarily lost interest in her faith. Although they did not condone the rebellious behaviour, they kept loving and blessing their daughter, and waited it out. With God-given authority over her life, her parents prayed in agreement that the pleasure of sin would soon be abated.

Soon after, when she disclosed her secret lifestyle, her parents' unconditional love helped melt her rebellious heart, and her life began to turn around. In fact, she wrote the following note to her parents to explain why even a blessed child can wander from the truth at times:

Teenagers have a weak point – fear. The devil pours into young girls and guys a fear of consequences, disapproval, and disappointment, especially in the teen years. I was overcome with fear that whatever I had done – whether trivial or significant – I would be ruined if I confessed. I always had my parents blessing, but fear kept me from understanding the great love that is a product of parental blessing. I was so bound by Satan's lies that I became a slave to my own deceit. Satan had me convinced that the last two people I could ever run to for safety on this earth, were my parents. In fact, nothing was farther from the truth.

When parents are walking in God's will and are blessing their children, there is freedom for confession. When I finally told my parents all that had happened, I felt more loved than ever before. The elation, when we run back into the arms of God and of guardians He has put over us, abounds to cover all sin. There is freedom in receiving and giving God's blessing. It is beneficial to let your kids know that no matter what they've done, you will receive them with love and forgiveness.

We know this story is true because this teen's name is Jessica, and we are her parents. Her life has never been the same since. After turning her heart back to Jesus, she led many of her friends to Christ. Two years later we had a blessing party for a dozen of them in our home.

Your story may be different from ours. You may have to endure longer than we did. But in the end, we assure you, blessing prevails.

We bless you

We bless your teen years. You have what it takes to fulfill everything God has called you to do. As you apprentice for adulthood, may your unique talents and gifts be recognized and stimulated in preparation for your life's work.

We bless your physical development, that you are content and happy in the body God has given you as it reaches maturity. May you enjoy excellent health.

We bless your mental development, that you receive the necessary education and intellectual preparation for your life's work. May you appreciate both the process and outcome of learning.

We bless you spiritually, that you may have personal encounters with the living God. May you experience consistent growth in your faith day by day.

We bless you socially, that you may experience true friendships, a good reputation, and a safe environment in which you feel loved and accepted for who you are.

We bless your life preparation. May these years truly serve as an apprenticeship period for adulthood. May you always be mentored in character and in your life's calling.

We bless your need to grow. May you learn from your mistakes and experiment with your gifts and talents. May you never fear to accept new challenges and test the limits of your capabilities within the boundaries set by godly authority.

Endnotes

[1] Jim Volvano was a recruiter, motivator, and the beloved coach of the North Carolina State basketball team. He died in 1993 at 47 years of age.

CHAPTER THIRTEEN

Adulthood

What am I called to do in this world and who will share my journey?

Jesus was baptized too. And as He was praying, heaven was opened ...and a voice came from heaven 'You are my beloved Son and I am fully pleased with you.'
Luke 3:22 NLT

We must do more than bring our sons into this world. We must also launch them into their manhood and walk with them every step of the way.
Brian D. Molitor[1]

"Heaven was opened"! What a beautiful word-picture of living in God's favour where God's presence is frequently felt and answers to prayers are frequently seen; where there is no barrier to open communication with a heavenly Father who is committed to our wellbeing; and where God's supply meets our every need (see Philippians 4:19).

Is it possible to live in such a world? We believe it is. And we believe that the blessing God intends for you to receive at adulthood helps to open the storehouse of heaven where all our spiritual blessings are waiting to be released upon us here on earth (see Ephesians 1:3). After all, God didn't intended for us to get by without His supply, or, as we like to say, a Christian's life should not just be "pie in the sky when you die, but steak on the plate while you wait"!

When you walk in your God-given destiny, you can expect God to open the heavens above you and give you all the resources you need to carry out your task. We've seen it happen time and time again. Unfortunately, not every follower of Jesus has been blessed to live under an open heaven, and as a result they struggle to prosper in life.

Len, a 30-year-old, came to our church for counselling. He looked the part of a successful man, yet he simply could not keep a job or a girlfriend for any length of time. The reason for his restlessness became quickly evident as he shared his story.

Len had just completed a house that he had built virtually by himself. Framing, electrical, plumbing – he did it all, but not just to save money.

When the house was completed, Len brought his father to the house site and gave him the grand tour explaining every detail of what he had done and how he had done it. His dad said nothing until the end of the tour. Proudly Len turned to his dad, "Well dad, what do you think?" His dad paused and then listed everything in the construction that his son could have done better. No praise, no affirmation.

Len buried his head in his hands and moaned, "I built that house all by myself just to prove to my dad that I could do it. Why won't he ever tell me I have done a good job?"

Blessing isn't a reward. It's a gift. When parents use blessing as a reward for good behaviour, they miss the point. When parents withhold blessing as a means of correction, punishment or motivation for their children, as did Len's dad, they reap unfortunate results. For Len, the heavens seemed like brass. Anxious and overdue to begin his adult journey, he longed to hear, That's my boy! from the man who mattered most in his life.

When the heavens open

Contrast Len's experience with that of another 30-year-old

named Jesus (see Luke chapter 3).

At the time Jesus' cousin John was at the forefront of a national spiritual revival as he led untold numbers through a baptism of repentance. The spiritual atmosphere was charged with expectancy that Israel's Messiah would soon be revealed. The magnitude of the revival was reflected by the fact that even unlikely candidates, such as tax collectors and soldiers, made the long trek to the Jordan river to be a part of what God was doing through John.

Jesus also made the trek and insisted on going through the same baptism as everyone else. No one in the crowd knew Jesus' true identity yet, but God used Jesus' baptism as the ceremonial backdrop for a heavenly impartation.

Jesus' Father had prepared a special time and a special place where to give His Son a blessing. As John baptised Jesus, the heavens opened above Him, and two things happened (see Luke 3:21-22): His Father extended "a meaningful touch" to Him through the manifestation of the Holy Spirit in the bodily form of a dove that landed upon Jesus and His Father spoke a message in an audible voice that "attached a high value" to Jesus saying, "You are my beloved Son in whom I am fully pleased."

Regardless of whether anyone else heard the heavenly voice, the words were meant for one person – they flowed directly from the Father's heart to His Son. The words, "You are," and "I am fully pleased," represented an unqualified affirmation upon Jesus' character. In essence the Father was saying to His Son, "I have watched your character growth and I am happy with it. I am proud of who you have become."

Jesus received this affirmation as a gift from His Father before He began His ministry. He hadn't earned it. He hadn't performed one miracle; He hadn't preached one sermon, and hadn't picked one disciple. Yet He was already walking in God's favour under an open heaven. His

Father's confidence in Him gave Jesus complete confidence that He was ready to fulfill the purpose for which He had come to earth. As we watch Jesus' life through the Gospel accounts, it becomes evident that He never lacked God's supply even for a minute.

In the same way blessing from our earthly parents opens the heavens above us.

When heaven opens over a blessed person's life, it affects every area of their life. Sometimes that effect is immediately evident in the form of material provision, like in the case of the man whose consulting business suddenly prospered after his mother blessed him (see Chapter 6). The parental blessing brought a new level of favour to the man's business and was a sign of God's favour – a supernatural boost to a credible business plan.

While the blessing of the Lord is bound to bring a measure of financial wellbeing in addition to spiritual benefits (see Proverbs 10:22), it does not always follow that blessing immediately brings material wealth. Prayers of blessing don't somehow exempt us from hard work, nor do they hold the promise for financial wealth that exceeds our talents. We simply have the guarantee that He will meet all our needs (see Philippians 4:19).

When ceremonies become celebrations

Jesus received another aspect of the blessing at His baptism. His Father not only affirmed His character, but John publicly announced Jesus' calling and coming ministry saying, "Look – the Lamb of God who takes away the sin of the world" *(John 1:29)*. This was a big event. Huge crowds of spiritually hungry people had come to listen to John. They knew he was preparing the way for the Messiah. Jesus could have received no higher commendation, and no one was more qualified to give it than John.

Ceremony was highly valued in the ancient Jewish culture, and much of that culture was directly instituted by God through Moses. A study of the Hebrew feasts reveals that God loves to celebrate. Would He not have desired to celebrate the inauguration of His only Son's ministry?

God the Father planned to stage the inaugural event in a remote desert region ensuring that only true God-seekers would be present rather than the merely curious. Those in attendance came a long way hoping that they would learn more about the Messiah. They were not disappointed. Having announced Jesus' ministry, John stepped aside and gave Him pre-eminence (see John 3:30). Jesus received the honour due His unique identity and destiny. What a celebration they must have had!

Our culture is not as focused on meaningful ceremonies. Among the few we have retained are graduation and wedding ceremonies. These represent excellent opportunities for imparting blessing to young adults because they mark significant transition points in life. A graduation embraces a life calling, and a wedding, a life companion. Both can be turned into celebrations that seal the blessing released into young adults' lives.

It works well for many family members and friends to speak into the lives of the bride and groom, especially for a first time marriage of two young people. Wedding receptions are ideal for speaking meaningful words that can be delivered in a public setting.

In our years of pastoring we have attended far too many receptions where a father or mother failed to use the opportunity wisely. We are incredulous to see embarrassed parents offer 30 seconds' worth of trite comments followed by awkward speeches full of attempted humour and devoid of meaning. Parents ought never to miss this opportunity to review a young person's life and to speak blessing over their future. In Chapter 16 we give examples of innovative ideas that facilitate the impartation of blessing during weddings.

We have also noticed that hidden hurts can remain in a person's life for years when family members or close friends fail to attend a wedding. Never underestimate the value of your presence at key celebrations in the lives of people you know.

When the young leave the nest

When Jesus left the site of His baptism, He didn't return to live at home with His parents in Nazareth. He was led by the Spirit to go a different direction.

It is Scripturally correct for young adults to leave their family home and launch out on a life of their own. For example, the Bible makes it clear that when a man marries, he will "leave his mother and father" and become one flesh with his wife (see Ephesians 5:31). The old English word used in the *American Standard Version* of the Bible is "cleave" which means "cling to." We have witnessed couples in their middle-aged years still hindered from union with their spouse because they are bound with emotional ties to controlling parents.

Our experience allows us to say we can't overestimate the value of ensuring that young adults are properly blessed as they leave their parents' home to establish a career and home of their own.

Parents need to communicate the following through blessing to a child who is leaving home for college or to be married:

- "God is with you" – opens heaven over their lives to enable them to prosper fully;
- "You're going to make it" – affirms the child's readiness to take on the world;
- "We're always here for you when you need us" – assures the child that the parent will be available for consultation.

Without this blessing most young adults spend their 20s in what we call trial and error mode – trying this and that while they learn to discover who they are and what they may be good at. When a young adult leaves home with these truths deeply embedded in their soul, their life dreams will not be constantly threatened by insecurity. They will not be detoured from their destiny while attempting to prove their worth or competence. They will be excited and eager to get on with the adventure that they know God has called them to live.

When parenting roles shift

During adolescence parenting roles shift from teacher to coach. When adult children leave their family home, parenting roles shift again – this time from coach to consultant.

There is a difference between a coach and consultant. A consultant gives advice when consulted. No unsolicited advice and correction! But too many parents won't let their children go and cripple their child's ability to embrace the future.

"blessing from our earthly parents opens the heavens above us"

A remarkably successful and bright young woman who was thriving in her career met with road blocks from a controlling parent. Her happy demeanour hid the turmoil inside. She attended a Blessings Workshop, and during a session Melissa felt to pray on behalf of young adults whose parents needed to "untie the apron strings." We were unaware of any visible results, but when we returned home that evening an e-mail awaited.

God used your session today in a powerful way. It is a watershed moment in my life. I feel God is releasing me

*into my calling and destiny to stand for truth and right-
eousness in my chosen field of work. My father was
absent during important times of my life and my mother
is rather controlling and has never fully released me as an
adult because of her fears and overprotective nature.*

*Melissa's prayer at the end concerning controlling
mothers who don't see what God is doing in different
stages of their child's life, related to me directly. So did
Terry's prayers concerning absent fathers.*

*I have renewed faith to believe that God is going to do
something different and powerful in my life in the coming days. It's so timely, since my boyfriend and I are
praying about marriage and even the possibility of
working overseas.*

The prayer of blessing brought heaven's perspective to
this young life and gave her the ability to apprehend her
own future with confidence.

When marriage partners need blessing

*"when marriage
partners are not fully
blessed individually, the
result will be a 'bent'
relationship pattern
with their spouse"*

It is more than just a
point of interest to
note that some of
Jesus' greatest opposi-
tion came from the
people who knew Him
best. Likewise, some of
the greatest challenges
we face come from
within our own home.
Unfortunately, those who enter marriage without sufficient
blessing in their lives often revert to patterns of dishonour
once the honeymoon is over.

When marriage partners are not fully blessed individually, the result will be a "bent" relationship pattern with their spouse:

- they will "bend" toward the other person and present them with their unpaid emotional bills from past hurts;
- they will "bend" away from the other person avoiding intimacy in a vain attempt to prevent further emotional pain;
- they will live in pretence looking and behaving like a normal couple while at least one or both are living a life of quiet desperation.

We call this state of relationship "married singleness."

In praying with couples, we have come to realize that marriage problems are often each partner's lack of blessing manifest in a close relationship. Once we understood this, we substantially modified our traditional approach to marriage counselling. If we led each partner to identify and recover their missed blessings, then health was usually restored to the relationship with little additional effort.

The real challenge is in helping people desire change at any cost – and there is a cost.

Part of that cost is a willingness to forgive. Whatever your family situation, healing entails learning to give and receive forgiveness and replacing embedded lies with the truth. Whether a parent, spouse, or a former spouse, we must let them off our hook in order to become candidates for God's blessing. Without forgiveness, heaven closes and blessing is blocked.

When trials come

Living under an open heaven is not to be confused with living a problem-free life. Jesus often experienced opposition and misunderstanding. Immediately after His Father blessed His identity, Jesus retreated to the wilderness and experienced an attack on His identity from Satan himself (see Chapter 7). As soon as He returned from the wilderness to His home town of Nazareth He experienced utter rejection, to the extent that people He had known all His life attempted to kill Him.

Likewise, when we are subject to spiritual attack through temptation or personal rejection by people who ought to treat us better, it is essential that we know deep down inside who we are in God and where we are going, in order to maintain our perspective. When that truth is embedded in our hearts we are much more successful at keeping lies out.

When dad can't speak the blessing

If our parents cannot, or did not bless us in marriage, can we be a good marriage partner?

The truth is that many of us won't hear, That's my boy! or, That's my girl! from our earthly fathers and mothers as long as we live. In some cases, perhaps through death or divorce, a parent is no longer available to give the blessing. Terry has a story to tell about a missed blessing:

Before I discovered the principles of biblical blessing I was teaching on the subject of emotional wholeness. I thought I had done a pretty good job. But when I was finished, a counsellor came to me and said, 'I can tell that you never received your father's blessing.'

I was stunned. How did he know?

Something in my message had tipped off this astute man about the unfinished business in my heart. One simple statement had uncovered an unfulfilled longing – an emotional 'loose end' that still required the touch of God.

Although my father was a loving and kind man, he never demonstrated a personal relationship with Jesus. He also died suddenly from a heart attack just one month after I was called into full time ministry. We didn't have a chance to discuss what God was doing in my life.

Ironically, my father had lived for more than 50 years without discovering the purpose why I had been placed on this earth. In spite of the many blessings of God in our lives and family, this emotional loose end remained buried and unresolved in my heart. It was an invisible yet influential factor in my emotional responses.

It was time to deal with it. Because the counsellor and I were friends, I was willing to give him permission to speak into my life. He knew from his own experience what I was dealing with and he did for me what someone else had done for him. In a simple ceremony that included meaningful touch in the form of a gigantic bear hug, he called me forth as a man of God, speaking words of affirmation based upon his knowledge of my life, and enhanced by direct insights given him by the Holy Spirit.

To quote John Wesley, I felt as if 'my heart was strangely warmed.' It settled something deep within. It was more than a heartfelt wish from a friend – it was a spiritual impartation deposited in my soul.

That one event was a key turning point, but it didn't finish the task. Since that time I have heard words of affirmation spoken directly to my heart by God's Holy Spirit and by others at key moments in my life.

Recovering the missed father's blessing in Terry's life has certainly improved our marriage and helped us to be much more understanding of those who struggle in this area.

Be encouraged, and receive the truth that God is not limited by your family faults. He can take you from where you are, to wherever He wants you to go. Ask for the grace and the courage to recognize and receive the blessings you have missed, and watch what it does immediately to improve your marriage and family relationships.

When someone you know needs an open heaven

We find great joy in helping others find the blessings they have missed, especially young adults who are reaching out for spiritual mothers and fathers in their walk with God.

Kristy, for example, is a vivacious young woman who discovered that the world was not giving her the answers she needed in life. Her drive for love and acceptance had led her on a fruitless search in many directions until she became hungry for spiritual reality. Our daughter's friend led her to faith in Jesus Christ. We then came to know her situation and realized that Kristy had not yet understood or received blessing on her new identity as a young Christian adult. She eagerly accepted our offer of blessing.

We knew Kristy well enough to speak words of personal affirmation upon her character and to picture a special future for her life. We also told her the meaning of her name and spent time praying with her. A couple of days later we received a card from her with these words:

> *Thank you for such an amazing experience.... I cannot tell you how much it meant. You have both encouraged me to find out who I really am, and... without those words of wisdom I would not be as overjoyed and content as I am today. Thank you again so much for a special day I will never forget.*

Something supernatural occurred in Kristy's soul. As we spoke words from our heart the dove of the Holy Spirit descended upon her heart with a magnificent and gentle touch.

Maybe a young adult you know is waiting for heaven to open. With insightful words of affirmation you can impart life-changing blessing to them and be the door through which heaven's deposit reaches their soul.

If you prayerfully provide the words, He will provide the dove.

We bless you

We bless your adult identity and your destiny in this world. May you discover and fulfill the purpose for which God sent you to this earth. May you meet and marry God's perfect choice as a life partner

We bless your relationships, that God would lead you to those who can mentor you, as well as to those who need to receive from what you have been given. May you never be without meaningful friendships.

We bless your marriage. What God has joined together, may no one ever separate.

We bless your children, that the generational blessing upon your family line would be passed on to them. May each child provide breadth and depth to your own life experience. May each one share your values in life and experience a personal walk with God.

We bless the work of your hands, that your industry and labour will bring the abundance necessary to provide for your family and to sow into other's lives.

We bless your finances, that you may never have to get by without God's supply. May you always discern and obey the requirements for financial blessing. May you live securely without need or fear of want.

We bless your health, that you may physically prosper and not succumb to sickness. May you prosper physically even as your soul prospers.

We bless your Christian witness, that you would carry with you the fragrance of Christ in all that you do. May your character and lifestyle be a witness to the truth of God's promises. May you have many opportunities to share your personal faith and bear much fruit as you continue to abide in the vine – Jesus (see 3 John 2).

Endnotes

[1] Molitor, Brian D. *A Boy's Passage – Celebrating Your Son's Journey into Maturity.* Unpublished manuscript.

CHAPTER FOURTEEN

Senior Years

Am I still needed in this world?

Her husband is respected at the city gate, where he takes his seat among the elders of the land. Her children rise up and call her blessed.

Proverbs 31:23

The glory of young men is their strength, gray hair the splendour of the old.

Proverbs 20:29

At the ripe old age of 50, friends of ours sold their business and moved to Africa to work as volunteer missionaries. The husband was prematurely gray. In fact, he sported a head of completely white hair, which brought instant respect among the people group they served. Not so in North America. The North American culture idolizes youthfulness and fears old age. Here he would have earned more respect if he had used Grecian formula.

Commercials promote a "Freedom 55" lifestyle of playing golf, cruising the Caribbean, or roaming the continent in an RV. When the house is paid off, vacations are longer, the schedule is free of work, and the question arises: *Am I still needed in this world?* A truly blessed life as a senior adult needs purpose as much as pleasure, and that purpose is found in relationships between generations.

Sitting in the gate

In biblical times people often lived in walled towns or cities. Many worked in the fields outside the walls all day and then came inside at night for protection. When people reached their senior years they were no longer expected to contribute to the city through hard work and thus ceased their labour in the fields. Now they were valued for a lifetime of accumulated wisdom.

Some seniors were given a seat of honour at the city gate. The city gates were a key location in the city because they provided a "courtside" view of all the action. City gates were for much more than just socializing. The elders of the city gathered there to oversee business transactions and settle disputes. Gatekeepers relied on the watchful eye of the elders to notice the comings and goings of all who passed through the gates, especially strangers. Seniors who weren't officially honoured with a position in the city gates sat in the gate on behalf of their families. They were invited to live with their families and devote their lives in helping the next generation succeed.

It is interesting to compare the biblical model for seniors with the life of Jesus.

After Jesus completed His life's work on earth, He returned to be seated at the right hand of God. He now rests from His labours, and is highly honoured for His sacrificial life. He occupies the highest seat of authority from which He keeps watch over the world and constantly prays for the saints who are His true followers (see Hebrews 7:25-8:1).

In basketball terms, those who demonstrate wisdom and faithfulness throughout their lives are like former players who ought to be given courtside seats for life.

They may no longer be playing the game, but they continue to experience the thrill of what's happening on the court and to offer advice to players when asked.

Contrast this biblical pattern with the position of seniors in our society. We expect them to congregate together and leave the rest of us alone to get on with our busy lives. Churches often consign seniors to separate social functions where they can reminisce about the "good old days" of ministry.

If seniors seem critical at times, perhaps it's because they once held vital roles but have now been discarded – very much like a former minister whom Terry met during a cross-country flight.

Over the course of a few hours the man revealed how much he disliked the large church he now attended. As a senior he felt he could not relate, so he chose to sit in the balcony each Sunday. He had become a spectator instead of a participant. His critical comments were a mask for his feelings. No one wanted to hear what he had to say anymore. With no one seeking his advice or counsel, this man felt disconnected and useless in his home church. What's wrong with this picture?

Whatever reasons there may have been for the leadership to ignore this man's potential contribution, it's tragic to see seniors sitting in the "balcony" instead of in the "gates." Ignoring such a wealth of life experience is dishonouring to those who have paid with their lives to acquire it.

Seniors need ceremonies
Ceremonies communicate a lifetime of honour and blessing.

When appropriate honour is given to someone who has poured their life out for the good of others, then a blessing is imparted and "closure" is brought to that stage of their life. It is a misguided idea that "doing something for the Lord" means you ought not be honoured or thanked. Too often we have dishonoured those who have laboured among us by not publicly recognizing their sacrificial service. As a result they miss receiving a crucial life-blessing and it hurts, whether or not they are willing to admit it.

When Terry was speaking at a leadership conference in

South America, one of the other speakers was an American woman who, with her husband, had been a missionary in a South American country for 39 years. During that time she had acquired a nation-wide reputation for raising up indigenous full-time Christian workers. Recently she had retired, but had returned with her husband to South America to speak one more time to the Christian leaders whom she loved so deeply. In a casual conversation, Terry asked what her mission board in America had done for her when she retired.

"I received a paper certificate from the head office that said thanks for your 39 years of service," she replied.

For four decades of fruitful service with nation-wide impact, the sending agency had failed to honour this dedicated couple with a ceremony, or any other public acknowledgment of their faithfulness. Unbelievable! Apparently the office clerk who filled out the paper certificate hadn't even included the name of the country in which they had served.

> "A truly blessed life as a senior adult needs purpose as much as pleasure"

Coincidentally, Terry had planned to teach the leaders how to honour seniors. On the last day of the conference, unbeknownst to the missionary couple, he organized an informal ceremony to make up for the neglect of the mission board.

Having invited the couple to the podium, Terry addressed the 200 attendees asking anyone who might have been mentored by this couple to stand. About 20 pastors and leaders responded.

Terry pronounced a blessing on the missionary couple, recounted their sacrifices, and praised them for the fruit of their labours, represented by those standing. Each leader who was standing came forward and spoke their own personal words of affirmation to the couple. The wife buried her head in her husband's shoulder and wept as decades of sacrificial love were finally honoured appropriately. Everyone in attendance sensed a powerful presence of God. Evidently heaven was in agreement with the decision to publicly honour these humble servants.

"Her children rise up and call her blessed..."

Honour and blessing go together. One gives rise to the other. And nowhere do honour and blessing have a stronger connection than in the relationship between parents and children. "Honour your mother and father," is the first of the ten commandments, and it ends with a promise: "You will live a long life, full of blessing" *(Ephesians 6:2-3 NLT)*. The virtuous woman described in Proverbs 31 was honoured by her children – "they arose and called her blessed."

These Scriptures tell us clearly that the initiative for blessing must shift from parents to children. It's up to the younger generation to initiate the words, deeds and ceremonies that firmly establish honour and communicate worth and value in the lives of aging parents. The results can be wonderful.

One way to take initiative is through the celebration of anniversaries. At the 50th wedding anniversary of Melissa's parents, family from all over North America were invited. More than 40 came, including almost every member of the original wedding party. Special touches included skits, pictures and our daughter modeling her grandmother's wedding dress.

During the renewal-of-vows ceremony we invited the honoured couple to stand at the altar as they might have on their wedding day. This time, however, they were surrounded by their six adult children who in turn were encircled by 18 grandchildren. Terry led the children in a responsive reading that began with the words, "Today we rise up and call you blessed." The blessing included thanking the couple for choosing a lifestyle of giving first place to their family for half a century. It ended with the words, "As you are less able to take care of yourselves, we commit ourselves increasingly to look after your needs."

After we imparted this blessing to them, we saw some immediate fruit in the spiritual lives of some extended family members who were restored to a personal relationship with Jesus Christ.

Unexpected fruit can result from children blessing their parents. Ron and Christine were engrossed in careers, teenaged children, and needs of ailing parents at the time the following events took place:

After attending a Blessings Workshop, wrote Ron and Christine, we resolved to bless our parents even though they didn't know how to express affirmation and blessing. The homes we grew up in were quite similar. We were both accustomed to stern looks, criticism and very little praise. Meaningful touch, words blessing who we were, words calling us forth as a man or woman of God, words spoken into our identities and destinies – these elements of blessing were almost non-existent in our formative years. Nevertheless, when our extended family gathered to celebrate significant milestones, we made a conscious effort to publicly express our gratitude to our parents and honour them for our godly upbringing, their support in our higher education, their hard work ethic, and so on.

Although we didn't see any change in our parents' attitudes toward us, we had planted seeds of blessing, and later saw the harvest.

A year later Ron's mother began to suffer with Alzheimer's disease and his father was diagnosed with lung cancer. This produced a softening in his spirit. He began to relate to Ron in a way that he couldn't before.

Ron was excited to finally be able to discuss his spiritual journey with his father. The topic had always been 'off limits.' They wept and repented for pain they had caused each other, and discussed their mutual grief over a wife and a mother who was not like she used to be.... Ron's father called for his grandchildren to visit him for the last time. When they came he spoke privately to each about his love for them and how proud he was of them. He gave them a life blessing.

Christine was also struggling with unresolved issues in her relationship with Ron's dad. After 25 years, and with time running out, she was fearful that he still could not receive our love.

About four days before his death, the Spirit of God led Christine to ask for forgiveness, and to release blessing and honour over him. His response was, What did I do to deserve great kids like you?' Finally God had restored what had been stolen from our relationship. We felt released to arrange a very honouring funeral and sing as a family by his graveside, 'Praise God from whom all blessings flow.'

At his funeral Ron's father was honoured by many people – from former refugees whom he had assisted, to elderly people with whom he had had opportunity to minister. We couldn't help but think how he had meant so much to so many people over the past number of years, yet he was more-or-less absent as a father and grandfather. However, because of the acts of blessing that we performed, much reconciliation and healing occurred.

We had closure, and we buried all resentments with his body. At the graveside with uncle, aunt and cousins we were able to model forgiveness, honour and blessing. We also used the occasion to bless our children by giving each one of them a family heirloom. God gets all the glory.

You are an eternal being. The choice is not whether you will live forever, but where you will live forever. It will either be in an unhappy existence eternally separated from your Creator and Redeemer, or it will be in the joy-filled presence of your Saviour Jesus along with the countless millions who have also chosen to follow Him.

If Christ is your Saviour, then what you do every day has eternal value and your life on earth is mere preparation for what follows afterward. An old Salvation Army saying referred to death as a promotion to Glory. The blessing we impart to those in their senior years not only lays to rest longstanding relationship issues, but also helps prepare them for their promotion.

We bless you

We bless your senior years, that you may maintain a place of significance and purpose in this world. May you be confident in knowing that you are needed and wanted by those of us who follow after you.

We bless your life's work. May you receive appropriate honour for your years of labour. May your contribution to the kingdom of God on this earth be recognized and blessed.

We bless your health, that your strength will match the length of your days (see Deuteronomy 33:25).

We bless your relationship with your children, that they may rise up and call you blessed. As you become less able to look after your own needs, may they be more available to care for you.

We bless your life transition from working in the fields to sitting in the gates. May you be sought out for wisdom and counsel so that your hard earned insights will benefit many in the years and generations to come.

CHAPTER FIFTEEN

What's in a Name?

For this reason I bow my knees before the Father, from whom every family on Earth derives its name....
Ephesians 3:14-15a NASB

If the words we parents speak to our children have the power of life or death, then consider the phenomenal power resident in the one word we speak to them far more than any other – the word they will hear through out their entire lives. I'm referring, of course, to a child's name.
Rolf Garborg[1]

Names bring blessing

Nothing is more personal than a name. It was the first gift your parents gave you. It will last your entire lifetime.

There is an inherent authority in the assigning of a name. God gave Adam authority to rule over the earth. Adam exercised that authority by fulfilling his God-given assignment of naming all the animals (see Genesis 2:19-20).

Parents exercise the authority God gave Adam by naming their children. Naming is part of the stewardship of parenting, and because it is a great responsibility, parents ought to choose names for their children prayerfully and carefully. A name can bless, or sometimes curse, the identity of a child before they have an opportunity to discover who they are in God.

In biblical times, names were chosen to reflect identity as well as to prophesy destiny. A person was given a name that was connected to their nature, for example, "Abraham" means, father of a multitude.

The blessing imparted by the name was so important to God that John the Baptist's father Zechariah was struck dumb until he wrote on a tablet, "His name is John." He then made a prophetic announcement about John's identity and destiny.

The ancient Hebrews demonstrated an understanding of the power of names to shape destiny.

In a period of time when Israel was largely backslidden, a couple from the region of Tishbe decided boldly to name their child Elijah, meaning "God is Great." We know nothing else about Elijah's parents except that they must have had great faith to name their child "God is Great" during a very low point in Israel's history. Whenever his parents addressed him, he heard them say, "God is Great"! Can you imagine what that sounded like when he was a toddler?

"God is Great – eat your breakfast"!
"God is Great – put your clothes away"!
"God is Great – play nicely with your friends"!
"God is Great – what a mess"!

No wonder Elijah had no problem facing down 400 prophets of Baal on Mount Carmel. When he had to prove that the God of Israel was great, and immeasurably more powerful than Baal, he likely shrugged and thought to himself, No problem – God is great! Then he turned to those present and said, Okay guys – pour more water on that altar and watch this....

Some cultures today still connect the meaning of names to a person's identity and destiny.

A woman from our church went to China to teach

English kindergarten. The first thing she did was to assign each child an English name to help them learn, and to make it easier for her to remember their names. The parents refused to allow it until she told them the meaning of their child's English name. If they didn't approve the meaning, they refused the name.

Although such attention to the meaning of names has not been part of North American tradition, many young families have discovered the power and blessing in prayerfully planning the right name for each child.

Colleen and Darrell, a young married couple, were called by God to serve as missionaries. Within a few short years their ministry was fruitful and their chosen career path seemed blessed by God in every way. At about 30 years of age, they had their first child whom they named Nathan – meaning, "gift of God."

> *"In Biblical times names were chosen to reflect identity as well as to prophesy destiny"*

Soon after Nathan's arrival they were expecting again. One day, Darrell died suddenly of heart failure. But shortly before he died, he had said to Colleen, "If we have a girl, I want to name her Janae," Hebrew for "God has replied."

For the remainder of the pregnancy, Colleen kept hearing the words, "God has replied." Six months later, back in Canada, Colleen gave birth to a girl and immediately named her Janae. For five years, whenever she called her daughter's name, Colleen was reminded that God had replied to her sorrow with life.

However, the testimony of a God who replies didn't end with Janae's birth. When Janae entered kindergarten, she asked God for a "daddy" for Christmas. Within a year Colleen had met and married a wonderful Christian man who adopted both her children as his own. Every time we visit this family and greet happy little Janae we remember that God truly has replied to the prayers of both mom and daughter.

Discovering God's purpose in your name

But how many of us had parents who named us with our destiny in mind? What if your parents didn't pray about their choice of name for you? God still may have your destiny written on the meaning of your name. We are amazed at how many times an apparently arbitrary name is given significance and meaning by God later in life.

One young woman revealed that her father left her mother when she was young and moved to another country. When she was 17, she was in a car accident while returning home from church with her family. Her mother was killed and she survived. She blamed the accident on her father and on the fact that he was not there. Angry at God and full of resentment and guilt, she had lost hope concerning her future.

In ministry to her we suddenly experienced a breakthrough. We discovered that her name means "delivered." As a result, we were able to declare God's foreknowledge of her tragic accident and His plan to deliver her for a purpose.

Seeing the connection between the meaning of her name and the tragedy, she began to believe there was purpose for her life. She forgave her father, released her mother, and accepted the path her heavenly Father had chosen for her. In the days immediately following, there was a noticeable change in her – she was more relaxed and happier. A few weeks later we received this letter:

> I want you both to know that the time you spent with
> me brought about tremendous freedom and healing in
> my life…. I really thank God that you were there…

because you allowed me to step into realms and places where I had said I will never go again. My eyes have been enlightened to God's great love toward me even when I thought I already knew it.

Her perspective on life was radically altered when she discovered God's hand in the meaning of her name.

The story of a pastor from South America illustrates this point as well:

He was born to his parents while they were out of the country. They were refused re-entry when they returned with their ten-day-old son because they had not yet named him. After much discussion, the border guard suggested they call him Philipe. They agreed, and recorded it on the required government form. Unfortunately, Philipe always felt that his name was meaningless because his parents had surrendered their responsibility of naming him to a stranger.

Today Philipe, a successful pastor with a thriving city-wide ministry, leases a former estate property and uses the various out-buildings as centres for church ministries. Philipe and his pastoral staff use the former horse stable as their office space.

One day Philipe made a discovery. He learned that the meaning of his name is "lover of horses." It changed his perspective on his name and his life. Here was God reminding him in a humorous way that destiny was in operation in his life from birth.

Names can hurt

Nicknames can be a blessing when they are used as terms of endearment, or for highlighting a positive characteristic or personality trait. However, most often the opposite is true. Little people have big feelings. Contrary to the old saying, "Sticks and stones will break your bones..." names can really hurt you. As one with the last name "Bone," Terry speaks with authority:

My parents were going to call their first child Stewart, until they realized that he would be called 'Stew Bone.' They named me, their second child, Terry, not realizing that I would be dubbed T-Bone.
The teasing persisted throughout elementary school – even the teachers got in on the act. It hurt. But I could dish it out in good form, and a few emotionally scarred adults can still testify to the unkind names I called them.

Author Rolf Garborg says he used to be called "Rough Cardboard." He knew of a dentist named Doctor Toothacher and another called Doctor Payne; a veterinarian named Doctor Slaughter; a Baptist missionary named Sprinkle; and a used car salesman named Joe Swindle. The names of real people we know from our childhood include Holly Wood and Chris Miss. Reliable sources also tell us they knew people who were actually named Iona Parrot and Faith Matters (the only person we know whose name is also a sentence).

The story that really scores is the one about the South American soccer player who was so excited to be a first-time parent that he gave his child the first names of all his fifteen team mates and registered the name. His wife filed for divorce when she found out what her husband had named their baby daughter. Likely either the mother or the daughter later applied for a name change.

The Bible records that God frequently changed a person's name to identify that person more directly with their destiny. Abram (exalted father) became Abraham (father of a multitude). Simon became Peter, which means "rock." And Jacob (the deceiver, or supplanter – one who takes the place of another) became Israel (one who strives with God and prevails).

"The deceiver" was likely very glad to have his name changed to Israel. This name change could have factored in his desire to prevent his son Benjamin from carrying a name that would have been a curse.

Of Jacob's 12 sons only two were born to Rachel – the wife he truly loved. The birth of Rachel's second son, Benjamin, was bittersweet because Rachel died in childbirth.

By this time Jacob was already Israel. He fully understood the power of names to curse or bless. Moments before Rachel died while giving birth to her last son, she tried to name him "Benoni," meaning "son of my sorrows." Although Jacob loved Rachel deeply he refused to let his son be named according to his mother's pain. Instead Jacob declared that his son would be named Benjamin – "son of my right hand."

Jacob's naming of Benjamin was prophetic because Benjamin grew up to be a strong warrior with descendants who were brave fighting men.

The story of Benjamin's naming also serves as a picture of how some people struggle with their sense of identity – one identity, rooted in the pain of circumstances; the other, undergirding the future and serving to define destiny.

When such a dichotomy exists the choice is ultimately ours. We all have pain in our past. We all have an identity from our heavenly Father. Which will we choose to identify with?

The meaning of your surname

Discovering the meaning of your given name may reveal a special aspect of God's purpose for your life. Research into the meaning of your surname may connect you with a fuller sense of generational blessings on your life. Rolf Garborg and his brothers spent years traveling around the world distributing Christian literature. Once, while in Hong Kong, his brother noticed the word "Garborg" beside two Chinese characters. Further investigation revealed that the two words "gar" and "borg" in Chinese mean, to spread over a wide area. Rolf asks:

Was it simple coincidence that when all of us were working abroad in the distribution of Christian literature we discovered the meaning of our name in Chinese to be 'to spread abroad' – or can there be more significance to our surnames than we realize? In either case, it was a great blessing to these three brothers to realize that every time someone called us 'Garborg,' he was naming the vocation God had given us. [2]

Redeeming a name

Perhaps you have discovered the meaning of your name, and it is not a blessing. A teenager we met was named after a cheese her mother had eaten at a party while pregnant. Her name had thus become a family joke. This young woman needed ministry and healing from the stigma of always having to explain the reason for her strange name. Others have struggled with the meaning of their name until God brought them a fresh perspective.

A woman named Wendy, which means "wanderer," took hold of a new sense of purpose for her name when she was blessed and released by our ministry team to help those who wander from their faith to return to the Lord.

In cases such as these, the Holy Spirit may lead you, with the help of others, to redeem the meaning of your name by discovering what purpose God has in that name, and to have a blessing pronounced over it.

We bless you

We bless the purpose of God in allowing you to be given the names that you have. May you discover any hidden meaning and spiritual significance of the names you will carry with you for life.

Endnotes

[1] Garborg, Rolf. *The Family Blessing,* p.81. Word Publishing. 1990.
[2] Ibid, p.87.

CHAPTER SIXTEEN

Blessing as a Way of Life

Bless and do not curse...do not be overcome with evil, but overcome evil with good.

Romans 12:13,21

With the peaceful working together of inter-generational families, a blessing is passed on from one generation to the next.... This working relationship is a challenge for today's mix of generations. It does not just happen.

Larry Kreider[1]

The most powerful kind of agreement

Whenever you properly bless someone, you enter into a partnership with heaven through the words of your mouth and the kingdom of heaven arrives on earth – just like Jesus said it would (see Matthew 6:10). The agreement between heaven and earth expressed through your words is limited only by the inventory in heaven's warehouse, and we can assure you, nothing is on back order.

The spiritual power released when you bless may even outlive your life on earth. Ken and Jane Raymer, close friends of ours who truly understand and live the power of blessing, learned that it could become a generational trend that stays in your family line for hundreds of years.

Ken discovered this while researching his ancestry. He traced his family tree back to the 15th century. One of his ancestors

147

named Abraham came from Europe to Pennsylvania in 1700 to save his family from religious persecution. Hundreds of Ken's ancestors have served the Lord and prospered in North America since that time. Among them was Ken's great great-grandfather who happened to be named Simon-Peter. The current of blessing has flowed for many generations in the Raymer family gently encouraging each generation to yield to the ways of the Lord. Many of his extended family now serve the Lord – some in full time ministry.

You can start a generational trend in your family:

- Separate yourself from negative family traits; repent for sins that have been passed down through generations. This will help ensure that your spiritual house is in order.
- As you come to understand God's desired future for your spouse and children, impart blessing to them.
- Invite grandparents to come into agreement with you and your spouse.

Follow-through on a breakthrough

We've noticed that nothing stimulates a desire to bless more than seeing blessing in action in other people's lives. A holy envy stirs up in people when they hear how someone else is blessed. Something deep within us cries out, Me too! To encourage and motivate you, we have compiled a series of vignettes on the power of blessing. We pray that your heart will be stirred to capture this spiritual power and to pass it on to the people you love most.

At the same time that blessing generated solutions to Ron and Christine's struggles with their parents (see Chapter 14), they made a decision to bless their two daughters and two sons.

They realized their parents had neglected to bless them in some areas, but they deeply desired blessing for their children, and wrote, "We believed that if we...continued to bless the identities and destinies of our four children, they would carry on this practice with their children, and thus break generational relationship patterns."

Their hopes of establishing their children in the practice of blessing were rewarded. Within two years, during a Christmas gathering, their second daughter presented each family member with a journal in which she had written words of affirmation and blessing. "What a treasure to be blessed by your own children," they told us.

A blessing "Time Capsule"
A young married couple in our church caught the vision for blessing their two girls. They planned ahead.

They designed and distributed questionnaires to their extended family asking them to record a blessing for their daughters' weddings. Their eldest daughter was only ten years old at the time. The mother sealed the responses without looking at them, and tucked them away for safe-keeping until the day they would be used as part of the ceremony at their daughters' wedding receptions.

Only a few months later the grandfather on the mother's side suddenly passed away. At the funeral the mother showed us the sealed envelope that her father had returned to her only a few weeks earlier and said, "My father may be gone, but he will still be able to bless his granddaughters on their wedding day."

Bar barakah blessing ceremony
Bar barakah is a term some use for a Christian adaptation of the Jewish *bar mitzvah*. Whatever you call it, having a ceremony for a new teenager can be an excellent means of bestowing blessing upon their unique individuality. It may also safe-guard them from inevitable attacks on their self-worth during adolescence.

Ceremonies do not have to be large and expensive. More important than the amount of money the family spends on the ceremony, is the parents' commitment to ensure that the right people attend and convey the right message to the young person.

Because the purpose of the ceremony is to welcome a young person into their future as an adult, it is essential to include adults who have a meaningful relationship with the child. Making a ceremony memorable for the young person being blessed is key. Parents who have planned a *bar barakah* recommend that participants do the following:

- Write a letter of commendation
- Provide a meaningful gift
- Attend the ceremony if possible
- Commit to pray for the young person.

Terry was invited to attend a celebration planned by a single mother for her 16-year-old daughter. The mother had rented a hall, filled it with balloons and food, and invited significant people from her daughter's life to contribute, including several important male figures. Terry's contribution was a short message from a Psalm that he applied to each stage of her life.

Here is the account of another single mother who took the initiative to plan a celebration for her 13-year-old son Jeremy. In attendance were his father, grandfather, uncles, mentors, friends, aunts, grandmother and sister.

I prepared a service to acknowledge the stages of Jeremy's life from infancy to toddlerhood, and into childhood. The service affirmed Jeremy's growth in stature and wisdom and recalled both the good, and not so good, memories from his past.

Jeremy himself performed some of the requirements for the ceremony. Connecting with his past, Jeremy chose to wear the traditional dress of his African ancestors at one point. We praised God with the drum, steel pan, organ, calimba and saxophone. Jeremy received symbolic tokens and monetary gifts. To God be the glory.

Even though a ceremony "seals" a blessing that has already been expressed in words and deeds, it is no replacement for daily words of affirmation and actions that back up those words.

A blessing party

After our daughter returned to her faith, God began to bless our children in such a way that within a four month period nearly 20 of their school friends were showing up at church. Most of them made a decision to follow Christ. We have had a lot of fun spending time with these new Christian adolescents and even becoming a spiritual mom and dad to a few.

Thus, when our son Mark turned 17, we decided to have more than a birthday party for him. We had a blessing party. We invited all of Mark's and Jessica's new Christian friends, and a dozen came. Melissa prepared a name card for each person, writing on it the meaning and the connotation of the name, and a related Scripture verse.

Along with typical birthday activities, we spent a few minutes teaching about blessing. Then with each young person we performed a blessing ceremony. We told them the meaning of their name, and applied it to what we saw in their character. We told them that they had what it takes to make it in this world, and that it is worth waiting for the right life partner. We also offered to be available for them, if and when they needed someone. We laid gentle hands on their shoulders and prayed for God to guide and guard their lives in every way. For some it was the first time in their lives that anyone had given them such affirmation. The cards and calls we received later revealed how much of a lasting impact this event had on these young lives.

Blessing in your church family

When we teach about blessing in a local church, we sometimes call the pastor, elders and their spouses forward to receive a verbal blessing from their congregation. We coach people, explaining how a blessing is given. If we don't, people often retreat into prayer-mode when asked to give a blessing. Some close their eyes and pray up a storm asking God to do everything for the person they can possibly think of. That's simply praying for someone. That's not the same as blessing them.

> *"The spiritual power released when you bless, may even outlive your life on earth"*

We model blessing first. With our eyes open we speak directly to the person about the good things in their life and the special future God has for them (see the five elements of blessing in Chapter 11). Then we invite them to come forward and speak directly to their leaders from their hearts. We also release them to picture a special future for their leaders and express their personal commitment to them.

Within minutes a sweet flow of the presence of God surrounds us.

At a particular Saturday evening leadership meeting, we had scheduled 15 minutes for the 30 people in attendance to bless their pastor, his wife and the eldership couples. Blessings flowed non-stop for more than an hour. The weary pastor and wife came alive with the strength of the words spoken to them (see Proverbs 12:25).

These examples are drawn from our experience ministering to church leadership, but there's no reason to stop there. This same kind of corporate blessing event can work with any group in your church.

Blessing a town

A pastor and his wife discovered the power of blessing, and got on a roll. They wrote, "We had just blessed everyone in the church, finding the meaning of their names.... We decided to do the same for the town."

Gathering ideas from the town flag, they wrote a blessing on a sheet of parchment and made an appointment to appear before the Town Council at one of their regular meetings.

"At the meeting we told them we were not there to bring a complaint, but to bring something much different."

The pastor's wife explained the significance of blessing, and the pastor read the blessing they had prepared. The Town Council inserted the blessing in a time capsule for the town's 75th anniversary celebration and hung another copy in the Council Chambers.

Innovations at weddings

People's hearts are usually open to new ideas for weddings and receptions. Some couples like innovation at a ceremony to make it memorable. Adding words of blessing to the order of events is usually welcomed as a novel suggestion.

A minister who heard about blessing from us was scheduled to perform his own daughter's wedding ceremony. He immediately modified the order of service to include a formal blessing. The father of the groom and the pastor took seven minutes of the ceremony to impart the father's blessing. The minister reported:

We followed the five elements of blessing as you had shared them. First we took turns speaking words of value about our children. Then we pronounced the blessing.

We laid our hands on their shoulders when we spoke (for 'meaningful touch'). We told the couple how we would partner with them on their journey. Then we presented them with a Study Bible that we, the fathers, had picked out together. We had had it imprinted and inscribed with calligraphy.

The blessing turned out to be an intensely emotional aspect of the ceremony. Everyone commented on its uniqueness and impact. The minister still reminds us of the powerful effect on everyone.

Grandparents stand in

Grandparents have spiritual authority and relational rights to bless their grandchildren.

While it's best for grandparents to work in harmony with parents, there are occasions when grandparents need to take the initiative. At times consequences of refraining from blessing can be too great. Be encouraged! Evil can be overcome with good, as we see from this personal story of a businessman who has made it his goal to practice blessing as a lifestyle:

I had the pleasure of helping grandfathers of two families design unique celebrations for their teenaged grandsons. Each of them did so under some heartbreaking circumstances. In the first situation, the boy's father had murdered his mother and was placed in prison for life. In less than one minute, the boy had lost both parents.

In the second situation, the boy's father had committed suicide, leaving the boy and his mother to face the chal-

lenges of life alone. Fortunately for the boys who were left to cope with the unimaginable, their grandfathers intervened to create powerful celebrations for their grief-stricken grandsons. In both cases the grandfathers reported that the impact on their boys was profound. It was as if a wall of protection was built between them and the tragedies of their recent pasts. [2]

Going the extra miles

We were touched by the story of a man who, after he received blessing and experienced personal breakthrough, went to great lengths – and many miles – to ensure his extended family received all that he had experienced.

The man had attended a men's retreat where the speaker had taught on blessing and had prayed the father's blessing over him. "So much pain washed away that day," he related.

For the next year he and his father enjoyed precious moments that had never been possible. The next summer the man's father died suddenly. "I am so grateful for the final year I had with him," he said. "I was able to speak blessing to him and to tell him I loved him. We had a family dinner at a restaurant that summer and I honoured him in front of my mother, my siblings, nieces and nephews."

As a musician the man had been writing songs for many years but "after the blessing came, the songs took on new power," he said. "The Lord even allowed me to write a song for my aunt and uncle's 50th wedding anniversary. I traveled more than 2,000 miles to sing it to them. It was truly a blessing for them and for me."

Try it – it's the best

A former professional wrestler – a new Christian – was becoming acquainted with the Bible and learning how to live his new faith, when he attended the Blessings Workshop.

"It is awesome!" he wrote. "I thought God was the only one to give blessings. Then I learned that I can give a blessing to my kids, so I started to bless them at bedtime. I found out that blessing works. Now my kids won't go to bed without a blessing. It seems to settle them down and give them peace. As I grow in God, I sure hope I can get better at this so I can bless my family and my Christian and non-Christian friends. *Try it – it's the best!"*

Dear reader

I call heaven and earth to witness this day against you that I have set before you life and death, the blessings and the curses; therefore choose life, that you and your descendants may live.

Deuteronomy 30:19

Blessing is a key to life (see Deuteronomy 30:19). This teaching didn't originate with Terry and Melissa Bone. If it had, then the best we could offer is to say it might work. Instead, we can say with assurance, this teaching unveils a Scriptural principle based on God's desire to see you flourish and prosper in the life and destiny He has planned for you. Blessing *does* work.

In this book we have limited our discussion to the seven stages of blessing on our identity and destiny – spiritual blessings that nourish our soul and enable us to "rule" wherever God gives us authority. Much more remains to be explored, discovered and applied in the biblical teaching of blessing. For example, we haven't touched upon the blessings God bestows for obedience (see Deuteronomy 28 and Matthew 5).

We encourage you, meditate on, and pray about the things you have read in this book. Then spend time in

God's Word, delve into the promises of blessing, and receive all that God has for you. Ask God to direct you in words of blessing to speak over your loved ones, friends, and others whom He brings across your path. As you discover and recover your missed blessings, your life will surge forward with new spiritual momentum that makes it easier to find and fulfill God's purpose for your life.

It's your destiny. It's your decision. Choose life.

We bless you

We bless your identity and your destiny, that you may revel in the truth of who you are in Christ and rule in your God-given area of authority.

We bless you to go and bless others! May you give from the overflow of having received more than you can contain.

May the Lord bless you and keep you;
May the Lord make His face to shine upon you
And be gracious to you;
May the Lord turn His face toward you
and give you peace.
We ask this in Jesus' name. Amen.

Endnotes

[1] Kreider, Larry. *The Cry for Spiritual Mothers and Fathers.*, p.7. House to House Publications. 2000.

[2] Molitor, Brian D. *A Boy's Passage; Celebrating Your Son's Journey into Maturity,* p.174. Self-published manual.

IDENTITY & DESTINY

Also available from Identity and Destiny Ministries

Power of Blessing Media Resources

- Power of Blessing Workshop on DVD
- Power of Blessing small group study guide

Live presentations by Terry & Melissa Bone

- Power of Blessing Workshop
- Men's, women's and married couples' retreats
- Church Leadership consulting – how to grow a healthy leadership team

To order these resources, or to book a live presentation, please contact:

Web: www.idministries.ca

Email: info@idministries

Tel: (905) 945-8710

NOTES